HEALTHFUL COOKING -Recipes for Optimum Health

Genesis 1:29

"And God said, Behold, I have given you every *herb bearing seed*, which is upon the face of all the earth, and every tree, in the which is *the fruit of a tree yielding seed*; to you it shall be for meat." (KJV)

Genesis 3:18

"Thorns also and thistles shall it bring forth to thee; and thou shalt *eat the herb of the field*;" (KJV)

Exodus 15:26

"And said, If thou wilt *diligently hearken* to the voice of the LORD thy God, and wilt *do* that which is *right in his sight*, and wilt give ear to *his commandments*, and *keep all his statutes*, *I will put none of these diseases upon thee*, which I have brought upon the Egyptians: for I am the LORD that healeth thee." (KJV)

HEALTHFUL COOKING

–Recipes for Optimum Health

Written by
DEBRA E. S. WILLIAMS

Edited by
Lowin A. S. Spence

Copyright © 2021 Debra E. S. Williams
Visit the author's website at www.debrawilliamsja.com.
All rights reserved.

No part of this book may be reproduced by any means, whether electronically or physically (photocopying, photographing, etc.) or stored on any medium for use or retrieval, except in the case of purchased eBooks and brief excerpts for articles and reviews, without written permission from the author.

The author makes no explicit guarantees or assertions pertaining to the use of this book or guarantees any outcomes resulting from its use.

Due to the dynamic nature of the Internet, any links or web addresses shared in this book may have been changed or updated after the publication of this book and may no longer be valid.

Any photographs, illustrations, imagery or depiction of people and final product used herein are for illustrative purposes only.

Cover Design: Lowin A. S. Spence

Books by this author are available on Amazon, through booksellers or by contacting:

Dr. Debra E. S. Williams MBA, ND
Medical Missionary & Healthy Lifestyle Educator
Health Director – Life, Health & Foods
Shop #7, 4 Springvale Avenue, Kingston 10, Jamaica, W.I.

Updated September 30, 2022

Table of Contents

PREFACE 15
BIOGRAPHY 17

Beverages 22
    ALMOND SMOOTHIE 23
    AVOCADO BANANA SMOOTHIE 23
    WATERMELON SMOOTHIE 24
    GREEN VEGETABLE SMOOTHIE 24
    SUPER GREEN VEGETABLE SMOOTHIE 25
    RED VEGETABLE SMOOTHIE 25
    PUMPKIN and APPLE SMOOTHIE 26
    GREEN JUICE from IN MY BACKYARD 26
    CARROT JUICE 27
    TOMATO JUICE 27
    LIFE SORREL DRINK 28
    LEMON GRASS and GINGER DELIGHT 29
    SUGARCANE LEMON QUENCHER 29

Nut Milks, Punch, Shakes 30
    ALMOND NUT MILK 31
    ALMOND RICE MILK 31
    COCO-NUTTY MILK 33
    PUMPKIN NUT PUNCH 33
    BANANA NUT PUNCH 34
    ALMOND MOLASSES 'NUT SHAKE' 34

NASEBERRY and COCONUT MILK PUNCH 35

NUT MILK 35

CARROT and SPIRULINA POWER PUNCH 36

Cereals, Granola, Oatmeal, Porridge, Puddings 37

OATMEAL MANGO and COCONUT DELIGHT 38

NUTTY BANANA GRANOLA 38

OATMEAL with BANANA and MOLASSES 39

BANANA NUT GRANOLA 40

FRUITS and NUTS BREAKFAST 41

PUMPKIN MILLET PORRIDGE 41

GREEN PLANTAIN PORRIDGE 42

RIPE BREADFRUIT, COCONUT and MILLET PORRIDGE 43

BUCKWHEAT COCONUT PORRIDGE 44

RICH COCOUNT MILK OATS PORRIDGE 45

ORANGE and ALMOND MILLET PORRIDGE 45

ALMOND MILLET PORRIDGE 46

COCONUT PECAN BREAD PUDDING 47

CORNMEAL COCONUT CREAM PUDDING 48

EASY LOW-CARB ALMOND BREAKFAST CEREAL 49

STRAWBERRY CHIA SEED PUDDING 49

BANANA CHIA PUDDING 50

AUNTY RUBY'S NO-SUGAR SWEET POTATO PUDDING 51

NO-BAKE AVOCADO, CAROB and SWEET POTATO PUDDING 52

DEBRA'S MILLET COCONUT PUDDING 52

MANGO CHIA SEEDS BREAKFAST PUDDING 53

GRANDMA WENDY'S MIXED PUDDING DELIGHT 54

CAROB-PEPPERMINT ZUCCHINI FUDGE	55
Pies	56
CAROB BANANA ALMOND PIE	57
PUMPKIN-RIPE BANANA PIE	58
SWEET POTATO SHEPHERD'S PIE	59
BREADFRUIT NUT PIE	60
ZUCCHINI LIME (unbaked) COCONUT PIE	61
Breads, Bun, Muffins, Pancake, Crackers	62
WALNUT FLAT BREAD	63
VEGETABLE LENTILS FLATBREAD	63
RIPE BREADFRUIT FLAT BREAD	64
BREADFRUIT and PLANTAIN FLAT BREAD	64
OATMEAL BUCKWHEAT FLAT BREAD	65
BARLEY COCONUT FLAT BREAD	66
GREEN PLANTAIN FLAT BREAD	66
OATS FLAT BREAD	67
SWEET POTATO BEAN OATMEAL FLAT BREAD	67
FLAXSEED FLAT BREAD	68
TOMATO CHICKPEAS FLAX and CHIA FLATBREAD	69
BANANA APPLE NUT BREAD	70
BANANA NUT BREAD	71
WALNUT (YEAST FREE) BREAD	72
VEGETARIAN PUMPKIN WALNUT BREAD	73
MOLASSES SUNFLOWERSEED BREAD	74
DEHYDRATED BANANA NUT BREAD	75
ARTISAN BREAD	76
QUINOA OATS RAISIN BREAD	77

RIPE PLANTAIN RAISIN BREAD 78

BANANA TAHINI RAISIN BREAD 79

RIPE PLANTAIN COCONUT CASHEW RAISIN BREAD 80

DR DEBS SWEET CORN COCONUT RAISIN BREAD 80

FLAXSEED RAISIN BREAD 81

ALMOND FLOUR BANANA BREAD 82

SWEET POTATO CORN BREAD 83

SWEET POTATO BUN 84

STUFF CABBAGE LENTIL ROLLS 85

RIPE BANANA RAISIN ROLLS 86

BANANA BREAD BREAKFAST MUFFINS 87

CARROT CAROB PECAN NUT MUFFINS 88

BANANA GINGER MUFFINS 89

PECAN COCONUT PINEAPPLE MUFFINS 90

BUCKET WHEAT APPLE COCONUT MUFFINS 91

APPLE OATS MUFFINS 92

SAVORY CHICKPEA PANCAKE 93

CASHEW BANANA OATS WAFFLES 94

FLAX OATMEAL CRACKERS 95

CHICKPEAS and FLAX BISCUITS 96

Desserts: Chips, Cookies, Bars, Balls 97

KALE CHIPS 98

BANANA OATS COOKIES 99

CASHEW BUTTER OATMEAL COOKIES 100

COCONUT ALMOND FLAX COOKIES 101

GINGER CARROT OATMEAL RAISIN COOKIES 102

GINGER OATMEAL RAISIN COOKIES 103

SWEET POTATO BANANA COCONUT COOKIES 104

ALMOND BUTTER COCONUT OATMEAL COOKIES 104

PUMPKIN SUNFLOWER SEED COOKIES 105

ALMOND and ORGANIC RAISINS BREAKFAST BARS 106

CAROB SPIRULINA COCONUT BALLS 107

PINEAPPLE SUNFLOWER SEEDS COBBLER 108

PINEAPPLE ALMOND COCONUT SQUARES 109

Creams, Chutney 110

HOMEMADE COCONUT JELLY YOGURT 111

NON-DAIRY BANANA 'Nice Cream' 111

PINEAPPLE ZUCCHINI 'Nice Cream' 112

SPIRULINA 'Nice Cream' 112

BANANA, STRAWBERRIES and COCONUT JELLY CREAM 113

CASHEW BANANA LEMON CREAM 113

OTAHEITE APPLE COCONUT CREAM 114

TROPICAL JAMAICAN MANGO CHUTNEY 114

Cakes, Brownie 115

VEGETARIAN RAW CARROT CAKE BITES 116

CAROB COCONUT BANANA CAKE 117

CASHEW VEGAN CHEESECAKE 118

CAROB MANGO VEGAN CHEESECAKE 119

CAROB COCONUT CAKE 120

ALMOND MIXED FRUITS CAKE 121

SIMPLE VEGAN CARROT CAKE 122

BLACK BEAN CAROB BROWNIE 123

Patties, Burgers, Loaves ... 124
- CARROT and NUT PATTIES ... 125
- IRISH POTATO VEGETABLE PATTIES ... 126
- PINTO BEANS and CORN VEGGIE BURGER ... 127
- KIDNEY BEANS BURGERS ... 128
- PUMPKIN OATS BURGERS ... 129
- OATS PECAN BURGERS ... 130
- GUNGO PEAS BURGERS ... 131
- LENTIL BURGERS with FRUIT SALSA ... 131
- PUMPKIN-SUNNY SEED LOAF ... 132
- CARROT and RED LENTILS FRITTERS ... 133
- LENTIL WALNUT LOAF ... 134
- MIXED PEAS LOAF ... 135
- CASHEW NUT CHEESE LOAF ... 135
- DEHYDRATED VEGAN ACKEE QUICHE ... 136

Flax Gel, Spreads, Cheese, Butter, Jams ... 137
- FLAX SEED GEL ... 138
- HUMMUS (CHICKPEAS) SPREAD ... 138
- CHICKPEAS (mock tuna) SPREAD ... 139
- CAROB ALMOND and HAZELNUT SPREAD ... 140
- ALMOND NUT SPREAD ... 141
- BUTTERY ROASTED CARROT and GARLIC SPREAD ... 142
- BETTER THAN BUTTER SPREAD ... 142
- CASHEW CREAM CHEESE ... 143
- BELL PEPPER NUTTY CHEESE SAUCE ... 144
- WHOLE GRAIN MACARONI and NUT CHEESE with BROCCOLI ... 145

HOMESTYLE SUBSTITUTE BUTTER ... 146

PUMPKIN SEED BUTTER ... 146

MILLET PUMPKIN BUTTER ... 147

ROASTED GARLIC BUTTER ... 148

ORGANIC RAISINS and SUNFLOWER SEED BUTTER ... 148

PINEAPPLE FLAXSEED JAM ... 149

FIGS and ORGANIC RAISINS JAM ... 150

Salads, Dressings, Salsa, Mayonnaise, Ketchup ... 151

PURSLANE SALAD with GRILLED CORN, RED ONION, and a CREAMY AVOCADO DRESSING ... 152

CRUNCHY TOMATO SALSA ... 153

CARROT POTATO DILL SALAD ... 153

HEARTY BEAN SALAD ... 154

CALLALOO and BROAD BEAN SALAD ... 155

FAVA BEAN SALAD ... 156

CURRIED CHICKPEA, SPINACH and ... 157

ROASTED RED BELL PEPPER SALAD ... 157

LIVE PLANTAIN SALAD ... 158

CAULIFLOWER and BROCCOLI WARM SALAD ... 158

BLACK BEAN AVOCADO PAPAYA MANGO COLD SALAD ... 159

BLACK BEAN COUSCOUS SALAD ... 160

BROCCOLI and ORGANIC RAISINS SALAD ... 160

GUACAMOLE (AVOCADO SALAD) ... 161

SPROUTED MUNG BEAN SALAD ... 162

FARRO GRAIN and CHICKPEAS SALAD ... 163

BLACK EYED PEA and PUMPKIN SALAD ... 164

GARBANZO BEAN and RAW KALE SALAD ... 165

- MILLET WITH ONIONS and PARSLEY 166
- BULGUR TABBOULEH with CILANTRO and LIME SALAD 166
- VEGETABLE SALAD with TAHINI HONEY SAUCE 167
- HERBY CARROT and GINGER DRESSING 168
- TAHINI HONEY DRESSING 169
- CHICKPEA VEGETABLE SALAD with CURRIED CASHEW DRESSING 170
- ORANGE ORGANIC RAISINS SALAD DRESSING 171
- ORGANIC TOFU MAYONNAISE DRESSING 171
- BASIL CASHEW PESTO DRESSING 172
- KALE and BEET SALAD with TAHINI ORANGE DRESSING 173
- GINGER SUNFLOWER SEEDS SALAD DRESSING 174
- LEMON DRESSING 175
- STRING BEANS with ALMONDS or CASHEW NUTS 175
- FRESH PAPAYA SALSA 176
- EASY SESAME CABBAGE SLAW 176
- CREAMY CASHEW MAYONNAISE 177
- HOMEMADE TOMATO KETCHUP 178
- HOMEMADE CURRY POWDER 178
- CINNAMON SUBSTITUTE 179

Soups 180

- BROAD BEAN and CARROT SOUP 181
- BLACK BEAN SOUP 182
- PUMPKIN SOUP with COCONUT MILK 183
- MIXED VEGETABLE SOUP 184
- CHICKPEAS and VEGETABLE SOUP 185

CALLALOO and SPINACH COCONUT SOUP 186

LENTILS and CARROT SOUP 187

LENTIL and SWEET POTATO SOUP 188

Sauces 190

SWEET POTATO SALAD in COCONUT CREAM SAUCE 191

CHERRY NASEBERRY ALMOND SAUCE 192

CHICKPEAS and SWEET POTATO in CASHEW CREAM SAUCE 193

CASHEW SUNFLOWER SEED SAUCE 194

LENTIL BALLS with CASHEW and SUNFLOWER SEED SAUCE 195

Stews, Stir Fry, Balls, Steamed Dishes 196

SWEET POTATO and LENTIL STEW 197

LENTILS and STEW 198

THREE BEAN or PEAS STEW 199

SPLIT PEAS and LENTIL STEW served with QUINOA and CALLALOO 200

QUINOA and CALLALOO 200

STEWED DRIED GUNGO PEAS STEW 201

GUNGO PEAS and TOFU COCONUT STEW 202

LENTILS and GUNGO STEW 203

LENTILS, RIPE PLANTAIN and STRING BEAN STEW 204

KIDNEY BEAN STEW 205

CURRIED LIMA BEAN STEW 206

SPROUTED LENTIL COCONUT STEW 207

VEGETARIAN CURRIED GUNGO (Pigeon) PEAS 208

LIMA BEAN, CARROT and PUMPKIN STEW 209

LIMA BEAN STEW with ACKEE 210

KALE, CALLALOO and PEANUT CHOWDER 211

VEGAN KIDNEY BEAN CHILLI 212

KALE with GARLIC and SESAME SEEDS ... 213

TOASTED COUSCOUS with GARLIC and SCALLION ... 213

STEAMED SPANISH NEEDLE and CALLALOO ... 214

CREAMY COCONUT KALE with ONIONS ... 215

STEAMED ACKEE ... 215

STEAMED QUINOA with PUMPKIN ... 216

STEAMED CABBAGE and CARROT CURRY ... 217

CURRIED BREADFRUIT DELIGHT ... 217

OKRA and GINGER COOKED JAMAICAN STYLEY ... 218

SWEET and SOUR CAULIFLOWER BALLS ... 219

CABBAGE CASHEW STIR FRY ... 220

QUINOA and VEGETABLE STIR FRY ... 221

MIXED VEGETABLE STIR FRY with CASHEW NUTS ... 222

JACKFRUIT BBQ STIR FRY ... 223

KALE, PAK CHOY and CARROT STIR FRY ... 224

ROASTED ONIONS with RED-SKINNED POTATOES and SWEET POTATOES ... 224

Dumplings, Rice, Bulgur, Millet, Almond Nut & Meat ... 226

VEGGIE CURRY with LENTIL SPELT FLOUR DUMPLINGS ... 227

LENTIL SPELT FLOUR DUMPLINGS ... 227

SPELT FLOUR OATS DUMPLINGS ... 228

BAKED COCONUT CHICKPEAS DUMPLINGS ... 229

DEBRA'S SWEET POTATO CASSEROLE ... 230

CARROT BALLS with SWEET and SOUR SAUCE ... 231

COCONUT CURRIED LENTILS and BROWN RICE ... 232

PINTO BEAN BROWN RICE ... 233

SEASONED VEGETABLE RICE	233
ACKEE SEASONED RICE	234
ACKEE LENTIL SEASONED RICE	235
CARROT WALNUT ALMOND MEAT	236
ALMOND NUT MEAT	237
ALMOND NUT MEAT served with FRESH VEGETABLE SALAD	238
CHICKPEA FLOUR TOFU	238
BETTER TO HAVE YOUR VEGETABLES STEAMED	240
AN OPTIMUM HEALTH COOK'S GUIDE	242
OPTIMUM NUTRITION	246

PREFACE

'Healthful Cooking–Recipes for Optimum Health' has been written to serve as a guide for preparing healthy, affordable, and easy to follow plant-based meals. This book is geared towards helping you to be a true' *Health Reformer*' under the guidance of God's Holy Spirit.

The background to this book comes from my diagnosis of breast cancer in 2012. Please get a copy of the companion book '**How I overcame Cancer using God's 8 laws of health**' to get the full story of that journey. After discovering a 3.5 cm malignant tumor in my left breast I had it surgically removed in May 2012. I later learned from the post-surgery Pathology report that the cancer had already spread to lymph nodes under my left arm. So, I decided to regain health with diet and lifestyle changes through a positive spiritual attitude, trusting in God, learning as much as I could about food and nutrition and a comprehensive focused detoxification programme. (No chemo poison, no radiation burning nor removal of my breast!)

Since this experience, I have been on a journey to help others to prevent cancer and other lifestyle diseases, including knowing Jesus Christ as their Great Physician, Lord and Saviour. I am writing these words in June 2021, and since the change in lifestyle and diet I have lost over 40 unwanted/unhealthy pounds. My mind is sharper and so much clearer these days and I have a ton of energy.

My meals since 2012 are comprised primarily of fruits, vegetables, grains, ground provision, peas and beans, nuts and seeds….and I give thanks to God and our Lord Jesus Christ for divine grace and forgiveness of my sins in breaking God's '**laws of health**' which is what caused the cancer in the first place.

It has been great working with many of you over the past nine years, (one-on-one in some cases), as together we created healthy and delicious plant-based meals in your homes and also in group settings. God our Creator gave Adam and Eve (our first parents), their diet. "**Genesis 1:29**, KJV: "And God said, Behold, I have given you every herb bearing seed, which is upon the face of all the earth, and every tree, in the which is the fruit of a tree yielding seed; to you it shall be for meat." and Genesis 3:18, KJV: "Thorns also and thistles shall it bring forth to thee; and thou shalt eat the herb of the field". His direction and design are still the best for optimum health.

8 Keys To Better Health

- Nutrition
- Exercise
- Water
- Sunlight
- Temperance
- Air
- Rest
- Trust In God

I sat down at my computer on November 11, 2012 and started writing down some of my favorite plant-based recipes with added health tips. I haven't stopped creating, cooking, writing and sharing recipes, scriptures and health tips since then. It has been an amazing nine years, since that first day.

I do pray and hope you find this book helpful, as you prepare your homes/lives for your **NEW START** programme (Nutrition, Exercise, Water, Sunshine, Temperance, Air, Rest and Trust in God). For more details on the full NEW START programme please purchase the book '**The Ministry of Healing**' by Ellen G. White.

So, my dear family, friends and colleagues, I pray God's richest blessings over your lives and your health, as it gives me great joy to share my journey back to health with you, through my recipe book with 246 healthy recipes.

First of all, let's start with some basics that just about everyone can agree upon when it comes to being the best healthy 'you', that you can be:

- Eat as close to nature as possible: consuming whole fresh fruits, organic vegetables, legumes, nuts, roots, grains and seeds.

- Eat less processed foods (better yet, eliminate processed foods entirely: that includes veggie chunks, can-processed veggie burgers, steaks, fake bacon and all that stuff – out!!!)
- Drink plenty of water: at least six to eight glasses per day. Less, if you are already vegetarian and eating lots of fruits and vegetables which are high in water content!
- Get exercise daily: walking is one of the best forms of exercise (30 minutes five days per week is great!)
- Rest: so often taken for granted, but most important for the regeneration of cells in the body!
- Read – read – read…about health and wellness: what you focus on directs your actions and that becomes a lifestyle habit! With information technology so advanced you can just about teach yourself how to become a Health Consultant. You can Google recipes, training seminars on health, videos etc!
- Spend time alone with your Creator God daily (read your Bible and pray): meet Him first thing in the morning and consecrate your day to Him. Give Him full charge over your plans, life, health, business/job, education, assets and family!!
- Do a full body detoxification, and clean the blood, lymphatic system, liver, colon, kidneys, and your external cellular environment.

I pray the Holy Spirit will be your teacher, counselor and coach as you embark on this journey to renewed/continuous health and wellness, eating healthy for your own good, and for the honour and glory of God – in Jesus' name and by His divine grace and power, amen!!!

BIOGRAPHY

Dr. Debra E. S. Williams is a full time Medical Missionary/Healthy-Lifestyle Educator and Health Consultant. Previously, she spent twenty-three (23) years working in the fields of banking, entrepreneurship, finance and youth development, both in the private and public sectors in Jamaica and the wider Caribbean. Since early 2012 she has ventured into the field of Nutrition and Natural health, where she works with persons who are afflicted with lifestyle diseases, and teaches disease prevention through seminars, home visits, healthy cooking and meal preparation workshops, health consultations, community outreach projects etc.

She is a nine-years breast cancer survivor (who refused chemo and radiation because of their known ill effects) and instead used adherence to God's eight (8) laws of health to recover from cancer – acronym: NEW START (nutrition, exercise, water, sunshine, temperance, air, rest and trust in God).

She has committed her life to teaching the 'Health Reform' message, as given from God to the Seventh-Day Adventist Church since 1863. She is a dedicated Christian and a member of the Seventh-Day Adventists Church, Ocho Rios, Jamaica. In October 2017, Debra completed her **Doctorate in Naturopathy** (2014 to 2017) with the International Institute of Original Medicine (IIOM) in Virginia, USA, with a specialization in nutrition and preventative medicine. She is presently the Health Director for Life, Health & Foods Wellness Center located in Kingston, Jamaica.

What is a Naturopathic Doctor? Naturopathic physicians combine the wisdom of nature with the rigors of modern science. Steeped in traditional healing methods, principles and practices, naturopathic medicine focuses on wholistic, proactive prevention and comprehensive diagnosis and treatment. By using protocols that minimize the risk of harm, naturopathic physicians help facilitate the body's inherent ability to restore and maintain optimal health. It is the naturopathic physician's role to identify and remove barriers to good health by helping to create a healing internal and external environment. - **Dr. Debra Williams**

For information on health consultation packages, she may be contacted at admin@mylifehealthfoods.com . Her website is www.debrawilliamsja.com .

Contact numbers: 1-(876)-974-8813, (876)-878-8867 (WhatsApp) or (876)-326-4650

Dr. DEBRA E.S. WILLIAMS, B.Sc., M.B.A, N.D
Medical Missionary and Healthy Lifestyle Educator
HEALTH DIRECTOR – Life, Health & Foods Ministries and Wellness Center

PLANT BASED

Recipes

to get you started.

"Food can heal. Food can be your medicine. Food has POWER!"

LET US START WITH A FEW THINGS TO STAY AWAY FROM

Here are *a few main ingredients* I have removed from my recipes, along with other items you should stay away from.

1. **Vanilla Extract**. I didn't know that vanilla extract comes from macerating vanilla beans mixed with water and alcohol. The Bible tells us to stay away from alcohol, and I do not recommend the use of alcohol. I can't use an ingredient in my healthy recipes that contains alcohol. Most of the vanilla you find in the supermarkets are artificially flavored with a very high volume of alcohol. Vanilla extract can be very expensive. At most supermarkets you will find the imitation vanilla extract very cheaply priced, which is what most people purchase, thinking they are getting real vanilla – *please beware!!*

2. **Yeast Flakes or Nutritional Yeast**. The MSG-like flavor of nutritional yeast is not from MSG; but from free **glutamic acid**, an amino acid that breaks from its chemical bonds in the protein chain during the drying process of manufacture. Furthermore, most of the nutrients that the nutritional yeast contains are from synthetic vitamins and minerals which were added to the molasses that was fed to the yeast.

3. **Liquid Amino.** This is made by treating soybeans with hydrochloric acid to create free amino acids. The remaining acid is then neutralized with sodium bicarbonate, which creates sodium chloride, giving it its salty taste. On the one hand, it is very high in sodium, thus increasing blood pressure. On the other hand, it has a large quantity of free glutamates to over-stimulate the nerve cells. Taken from the book "**In My Backyard: Powerful herbs & foods of the Caribbean, Part 2, pg. 18**".

   I don't use this ingredient at all. However, because of its popular use among vegetarians and vegans, I will feature it under this section for your edification. **Soy Protein Isolate** is derived from soybeans. It has one of the highest concentrations of **glutamic acid** when compared to other high protein foods. For every 100 g of soy protein, there is 17g of glutamic acid. Textured Vegetable Protein (*Veggie Chunks or Mince*), powdered soy milk and most boxed soy milk have soy protein isolate as their based.

4. Why is free **glutamic acid** added in vast amounts to processed foods? Well manufactures have found that manufactured free glutamic acid, in the form of **monosodium glutamate (MSG)**, hydrolyzed vegetable proteins, textured vegetable protein, whey, natural flavor, malt extract, bouillon, broth, stock flavoring, natural chicken or beef flavoring, yeast extract, nutritional yeast, sodium caseinate, calcium caseinate, Carrageenan and anything with glutamate, when added to their processed food products, masks off flavors and makes the blandest and cheapest foods taste wonderful.

   The story is fascinating. For thousands of years Kombu and other seaweeds have been added to foods in Japan to enhance flavor. In 1908 a Japanese scientist discovered that the active ingredient in Kombu is glutamic acid and then the use of its sodium salt, monosodium glutamate, began in Japan. During the Second World War American quartermasters realized that Japanese army rations tasted great. Following the war, they introduced monosodium glutamate, the flavor enhancing ingredient in the Japanese rations, to the food industry; and the world-wide use of processed free glutamic acid began to explode.

Read more: http://americannutritionassociation.org/newsletter/free-glutamic-acid-msg-sources-dangers

Glutamic acid is a neurotransmitter that excites our neurons (*not just in our tongues*). This electrical charging of neurons is what makes foods with added free glutamic acid taste so good. Unfortunately, the free glutamic acid can cause problems in many people. Actually, our brains have many receptors for glutamic acid and some areas, such as the **hypothalamus**, do not have an impermeable blood-brain barrier. So free glutamic acid from food sources can get into the brain, injuring and sometimes killing neurons. Glutamic acid is widely distributed in proteins. When we eat it bound as part of whole, unprocessed proteins, it helps nourish us as it has for millennia. Glutamic acid bound as part of whole, unprocessed protein does not cause problems in people who react to the free glutamic acid in manufactured food, where it is **hidden in ingredients with about 40 different names.**

Monosodium glutamate and other forms of free glutamic acid can be manufactured cheaply and sometimes it is even just a byproduct of other food processes. For example, the brewer's yeast from the brewing industry contains free glutamic acid. Since free glutamic acid is cheap and its neurotoxic nerve stimulation enhances so wonderfully the flavor of basically bland and tasteless foods, such as many low-fat and vegetarian foods, manufacturers are eager to go on using it and **do not want the public to realize any of the problems.**

Scientists studying retinal degeneration in mice treated with free glutamic acid have noted that these mice also became **grotesquely obese** following administration of free glutamic acid. The vulnerable hypothalamus in our brains regulates weight control, as well as other endocrine functions. When the brain is deluged with more free glutamic acid than it can handle, scientists know that problems and diseases can develop. For example, they know that a diverse number of disease conditions such as **ALS (amyotrophic lateral sclerosis, a progressive degeneration of neurons and motor cells of the brain), Alzheimer's disease, seizures, and stroke** are associated with the glutamate cascade. http://americannutritionassociation.org/newsletter/free-glutamic-acid-msg-sources-dangers

Today, free glutamic acid is ubiquitous in processed food. What should we do?
- As individuals, **we need to consume natural, unfermented, unadulterated, unprocessed protein.**
- For everyone everywhere, we need to communicate with our friends, neighbors and relatives, our local newspapers, through the Internet about the danger of consuming MSG and now the common practice of misleading food labeling, so people will not know what they are consuming.

5. Now this ingredient in commercial bread, I just found out about early 2016 and the information, hastened my resolve to learn how to make my own bread and stop buying bread and biscuits from supermarkets! It is called **Cysteine. Cysteine** is made from the hydrolization (*a chemical reaction*

in which a compound reacts with water to produce other compounds) of **poultry feathers and human hair** and is used primarily for the creation of artificial flavors. When reacted with sugar, it produces a savory meaty flavor. It makes hydrolyzed protein and many meat analogues (*veggie meat products*) and is found in some bread as dough conditioner. **Cysteine** easily penetrates the intact blood-brain barrier and is linked to Alzheimer's and Parkinson's diseases.

6. **Soy Sauce** is made from fermented soybeans. Fermented substances are not recommended for dietary purposes and are linked to the development of cancer.

7. Vitamin Supplements

    Vitamins, vitamins, vitamins. Whether we get them from our daily diet, from sunshine, or from store bought capsules or liquids, vitamins are vital to our health and to the proper functioning of our bodies. Vitamin deficiencies lead to a wide range of problems spanning from anorexia to obesity, organ malfunction, confusion, depression and fatigue. However, whether or not your vitamins in a bottle are hurting you is another story. What people are not aware of is all vitamins are not created equal, and most are actually synthetic.

    ### What is a "Synthetic" Vitamin?
    The type of vitamins that are the most beneficial is up for debate. A healthy, **organic diet** should provide a good amount of nutrients that the body needs, but supplements can help ensure that we are getting a healthy serving of specific vitamins.

    The problem is that many vitamin and mineral supplements are manufactured synthetically with chemicals and do not come straight from their natural sources. They are made to mimic the way natural vitamins act in our bodies. Natural vitamins are derived directly from plant material containing the vitamin, not produced in a test tube. No matter which type of vitamin you choose, do not take one that contains high doses of any nutrients. According to the Academy of Nutrition and Dietetics, taking mega-doses of vitamins and minerals may harm your health and may increase your risk of heart disease and cancer. While organic vitamin supplements are safe as long as you're not getting too much, *if you're concerned about where your vitamins come from*, you may want to consider getting them from real food. There are nutrients in food that you can't put into a bottle. A healthy diet that includes food choices from all the food groups, including fruits, vegetables, grains and proteins, should give you what your body needs, plus the added benefits of phytochemicals, fiber, protein and healthy fats – **Dr. Edward Group** - http://www.globalhealingcenter.com/natural-health/synthetic-vs-natural-vitamins/

Beverages

12 Recipes

ALMOND SMOOTHIE

INGREDIENTS:
- Almond meal or pulp (*see almond milk recipe*)
- Almond milk
- 1 banana
- 1 papaya
- 1 cup coconut water
- pumpkin seeds, sunflower seeds and organic raisins

DIRECTIONS:
1. Place all ingredients in a blender and blend until smooth.
2. Chill in the fridge for a few minutes and then drink.

AVOCADO BANANA SMOOTHIE

INGREDIENTS:
- 1 medium avocado
- ¼ cup sunflower seeds
- 3 Tbsps. sesame seeds
- 2 cups pure or coconut water
- ¼ tsp sea salt
- 2 Tbsps. raw honey or maple syrup
- 1 tsp black strap molasses
- 1 ripe banana

DIRECTIONS:
1. Place the sunflower seeds, sesame seeds and water in a blender.
2. Blend to create your sunflower milk.
3. Add the remaining ingredients and blend until smooth.
4. Chill in refrigerator for 20 minutes and enjoy!

WATERMELON SMOOTHIE

Watermelon is 95% water and extremely alkaline-forming in the body. Eat separately and wait 30 minutes before eating something else. It is a very good source of potassium and is the lycopene leader among fresh fruits and vegetables.

INGREDIENT:
- watermelon

DIRECTIONS:
1. Slice a nice chunk of watermelon (*do not remove skin or seeds*).
2. Cut into small pieces.
3. Place in the blender (*no water necessary*).
4. Blend until smooth.
5. Drink right away.

GREEN VEGETABLE SMOOTHIE

(*STEAM and COOL ALL VEGETABLES. Refer to article on page 183.*)

INGREDIENTS:
- ½ head large bunch (*or ¾ small bunch*) organic spinach or callaloo (*steamed and cooled*)
- 1 small head organic romaine lettuce chopped
- ⅓ bunch organic parsley
- ½ organic lemon juiced
- 3–4 organic celery stalks
- 1 cup coconut water
- ½ cup water cress

DIRECTIONS:
1. Add the coconut water and chopped head of romaine and spinach to the blender.
2. Starting the blender on a low speed, mix until smooth.
3. Gradually moving to higher speeds, add the celery, water cress, parsley and lemon juice.

SUPER GREEN VEGETABLE SMOOTHIE

INGREDIENTS:
- ½ cup washed kale (*steamed and cooled*)
- ½ cup washed broccoli (*steamed and cooled*)
- ½ cup washed spinach (*steamed and cooled*)
- 1 tsp spirulina powder
- 1 tsp chlorella powder
- 1 tsp wheat grass powder
- Combination of ground seeds (*1 tsp each: flaxseed, sesame seeds, pumpkin seeds and sunflower seeds*)
- 1 cup coconut/plain water
- 1 tsp cilantro herb
- ¼ cup coconut jelly (*optional*)
- Dash cayenne pepper (*optional*)

DIRECTIONS:
1. Put all ingredients into blender and blend until smooth. Drink as a meal replacement or have 30 minutes before a cooked meal.

RED VEGETABLE SMOOTHIE

Don't allow your vegetable smoothies to sit for more than an hour, because the minerals and enzymes start to break down quickly once they have been processed!

INGREDIENTS:
- 1 cup spring or purified or coconut water
- A small piece of ginger peeled
- ½ small beet root (*steamed and cooled*)
- 2 carrots (*steamed and cooled*)

DIRECTIONS:
1. Place all ingredients in a blender (*add ice if desired*).
2. Blend until smooth.
3. Pour into a glass.
4. Drink within an hour of making.

PUMPKIN and APPLE SMOOTHIE

This smoothie can be a breakfast meal.

INGREDIENTS:
- 2 cups uncooked pumpkin (*chopped up into chunks*)
- 2 cups apple juice (*best to use fresh apples*) or Mott's cold pressed organic apple juice
- ½ cup of pineapple juice (*optional*)
- 1 tsp honey (*more or less to your liking*)
- Coriander powder and ginger to taste

DIRECTIONS:
1. Place all ingredients in a blender and blend until smooth.
2. Chill in the fridge for a few minutes and then drink.

GREEN JUICE from IN MY BACKYARD

(*STEAM and COOL ALL VEGETABLES. Refer to article on page 183.*)
Cucumber is a neutral fruit that can be combined with vegetables.

INGREDIENTS:
- 2 cucumbers
- 3 Spanish needle (*Biden Pilosa*) stalks
- 3–4 medium callaloo stalks
- Handful of moringa leaves
- 1 head of Pak Choi
- 3 parsley stalks
- 1-inch ginger

DIRECTIONS:
1. Wash vegetables thoroughly.
2. Cut into appropriate pieces.
3. Pass all ingredients through a juice extractor.
4. Mix and enjoy chilled.

CARROT JUICE

I don't recommend sweeteners especially when you consider that carrot is a very sweet vegetable – but some people can't take the straight carrot at first when they switch to a vegetarian or health reform diet – so use the sweetener until you can put it away.

INGREDIENTS:
- 3 pounds carrot
- Agave sweetener or honey
- 1 tsp lime juice

DIRECTIONS:
1. Extract the juice from the carrot in a juice extractor.
2. Add sweetener to the extracted juice.
3. Add lime juice
4. Stir well and enjoy.

TOMATO JUICE

You can be as creative as you wish in your own kitchen with any of the four options!

INGREDIENTS:
Option 1: Tomatoes, Bell Pepper, Celery, Ginger Root and Garlic.
Option 2: Tomatoes, Cucumber and Celery.
Option 3: Tomatoes, Zucchini and Asparagus.
Option 4: Tomatoes, Pineapple and Orange.

DIRECTIONS:
1. Wash thoroughly.
2. Cut into appropriate pieces.
3. Pass all ingredients through a juice extractor.
4. Mix and enjoy chilled.

LIFE SORREL DRINK

Do not throw away the pulp that is left over after you strain the sorrel – take the pulp, place in the blender, add organic raisins and a dash of coriander and cardamom and two tablespoons of agave or maple syrup and use as a spread to eat with your homemade bread or crackers!!!

INGREDIENTS:
- 1-pound sorrel
- 2–4 oz. ginger
- 2 quarts' sugar cane juice or water with maple syrup or agave syrup to sweeten
- 8–12 pimento grains (*optional*)

DIRECTIONS:
1. Wash sorrel thoroughly, using the fingers to lift it from the water.
2. Place into blender.
3. Scrape and wash ginger, cut into small pieces and add to the sorrel.
4. Pour in sugar cane juice.
5. Blend for about 5–10 minutes.
6. Allow to stand 4–6 hours.
7. Strain. (*Add pimentos in overnight. Remove next Morning, if using*.).
8. Serve chilled no need to add any ice.

LEMON GRASS and GINGER DELIGHT

INGREDIENTS:
- 1 tsp wet sugar or raw honey or maple syrup to taste
- ¼ cup lemon grass chopped
- 1-inch ginger peeled
- 2 cups pure water

DIRECTIONS:
1. Boil ginger in water.
2. Add lemon grass and steep until cool.
3. Sweetened, strained and drink.

SUGARCANE LEMON QUENCHER

INGREDIENTS:
- 1 stick sugarcane
- 1 Tbsp. ginger chopped
- Lemon juice to taste

DIRECTIONS:
1. Peel skin from sugarcane and chop it into small pieces.
2. Transfer all ingredients to blender and blend until mixture is smooth.
3. Juice out puree with your hands, strain it into a glass and refrigerate it for a few hours. Serve chilled.

Nut Milks, Punch, Shakes

10 Recipes

ALMOND NUT MILK

Almond milk is a beverage made from ground almonds, often used as a substitute for milk. Unlike animal milk, almond nut milk contains no cholesterol or lactose. As it does not contain any animal products, it is suitable for vegans and vegetarians who abstain from dairy products. Almond milk can be made at home by combining ground almonds with water or coconut water in a blender. Natural sweeteners are often added.

INGREDIENTS:
- 1 cup raw soaked almonds not roasted
- 2 cups coconut or purified spring water

DIRECTIONS:
1. Place all ingredients in a blender and blend until smooth.
   (You can add two tablespoons of raw honey or four dates to sweeten).
2. Strain and place in the fridge. This can last for two to three days. (*You can also add **sesame seeds** to the almond milk because they are high in calcium*).

ALMOND RICE MILK

Almond Rice Milk will last 4-5 days in the refrigerator. Shake well before serving.

INGREDIENTS:
- ½ cup almond soaked
  (*Peel off outer coat of nut – optional*)
- ½ cup cooked brown rice
- ¼ tsp. sea salt
- 1 Tbsp. raw honey
- 3 cups water

DIRECTIONS:
1. Place all ingredients into blender.
2. Blend until creamy for about 1 minute.
3. Pour in a glass jar and store in refrigerator.

PUMPKIN SEEDS and COCONUT MILK

Coconut Milk is a wonderful alternative to pasteurized cow's milk or to rice, soy or other processed milks. I don't recommend the dried packaged coconut milk powder because they contain added glucose, artificial sweeteners, and preservatives. Fortunately, making coconut milk at home is simple and very inexpensive. It can be used in smoothies, recipes, or just to drink by itself. It can also be flavored with natural fruits, carob powder or used to make other combination nut milk like almond or coconut, sesame seeds or coconut, cashew, or coconut etc.

Coconut is packed with medium chain fatty acids and lauric acid. It has many health promoting benefits and is especially good for children.

INGREDIENTS:
- 4 cups water
- 1 ½ –2 cups coconut shredded or diced
- 1 cup pumpkin seeds shelled
- 1 tsp raw honey
- Dash sea salt

DIRECTIONS:
1. Heat water, but don't boil. It should be hot, but not scalding. (*Warming the water helps to extract more milk*).
2. Place coconut in blender or Vitamix.
3. Add water (*If water is too much, add in two batches*).
4. Blend on high for several minutes until thick and creamy.
5. Pour through a mesh colander or strainer first to get most of the coconut out, and then squeeze through a towel or several thicknesses of cheesecloth to get remaining pieces of coconut out.
6. If you have to split the water, place all the coconut that you strained out back in the blender, add the remaining water, and repeat steps 4 and 5.
7. After all the coconut has been strained out add pumpkin seeds and blend until smooth.
8. Add raw honey and sea salt to taste.
9. Drink immediately or store in fridge.

(For best flavor and texture use within 3 – 4 days. Since there are no preservatives or fillers, the "cream" of the coconut milk may separate to the top if stored in fridge. Just shake or stir before using).

COCO-NUTTY MILK

INGREDIENTS:
- 1 cup coconut milk
- 1 cup warm water
- ¼ cup cashews or almonds
- ¼ tsp salt
- ¼ cup roasted oats
- 1 Tbsp. raw honey or hand full of organic raisins
- ¼ cup sesame seeds

DIRECTIONS:
1. Blend all ingredients until smooth.
2. Serve with cereal or have as a healthy breakfast or lunch beverage.

PUMPKIN NUT PUNCH

Pumpkin Nut punch is a very refreshing and nutritious beverage when served chilled.

INGREDIENTS:
- 6 cups water
- 2 cups pumpkin diced raw or steamed
- ½ cup cashew
- ½ cup almond
- Honey to taste
- Sea salt (*optional*)
- ¼ tsp. coriander powder

DIRECTIONS:
1. Dice pumpkin and boil in 3 cups water for five minutes (*optional for boiling, can be used raw*).
2. Blend until smooth with cashew and almond.
3. Add remaining water, honey, coriander, and salt to taste.

BANANA NUT PUNCH

INGREDIENTS:
- 2 cups water
- 3 ripe bananas
- ¼ cup roasted oats
- ¼ cup roasted peanuts
- ¼ cup almonds and/or cashews
- 1 tsp coriander powder
- 2 Tbsps. raw pumpkin seeds
- 2 Tbsps. sunflower seeds
- Sea salt to taste

DIRECTIONS:
1. Blend nuts in 2 cups water.
2. Add remaining ingredients and continue blending until smooth.
3. Serve chilled.

ALMOND MOLASSES 'NUT SHAKE'

Almond Molasses 'Nut shake' is delicious on hot or cold cereal. It can also be consumed alone for a healthy morning or afternoon beverage.

INGREDIENTS:
- 1 cup almonds soaked and blanched
- 4 cups pure water
- 1 tsp honey or maple syrup
- ⅛ tsp sea salt to taste
- 1 tsp molasses
- 4 Tbsps. sesame seeds

DIRECTIONS:
1. Blanch–soaked almond. (*Pour boiling water over nuts. Wait one minute, drain, remove skin by rubbing between fingers*).
2. Blend all ingredients in blender (*using half of the water*) 2–3 minutes, until smooth and creamy.
3. Add remaining water and blend again.

NASEBERRY and COCONUT MILK PUNCH

INGREDIENTS:
- 2 cups water
- 1 cup dried coconut diced
- 2 large ripe naseberries
- 2 Tbsps. sunflower seeds
- 1/8 tsp. sea salt

DIRECTIONS:
1. Blend coconut and water until smooth. Strain with cheese cloth or strainer to remove liquid from pulp.
2. Pour liquid back in blender and add sunflower seeds, salt and naseberries (*with or without skin*).
3. Let chill in fridge for approximately 15 minutes.
4. Have by itself as a healthy beverage or serve with home-made cereal for breakfast or lunch.

NUT MILK

NATURAL FOOD FORMULAS for Babies and by extension the entire family. Beverage for babies who are weaned from breast (*not intended to replace mother's milk*). Nurse as long as possible, weaning should be gradual; usually 12-18 months, baby should have a good start in life.

INGREDIENTS:
- 1 cup almond washed and soaked overnight
- 4 cups pure water
- 3 Tbsps. maple syrup or raw honey
- ¼ tsp. lecithin (*optional but it does make the nut milk creamier*)
- Few grains Celtic or Himalayan Sea salt (*has over 84 minerals*)
- ½ cup cashew or sesame seeds
- 2 Tbsps. sesame tahini
- 4 cups coconut

DIRECTIONS:
1. Add all ingredients in a blender using half the amount of water, gradually adding remaining water while blending until smooth.

2. Put through a fine strainer into glass, cup, or bottle.
3. Pulp may be added to cereals, bread, or homemade cookies.

CARROT and SPIRULINA POWER PUNCH

INGREDIENTS:
- 5 carrots washed
- 1 Tbsp. spirulina
- 1-inch piece ginger
- 1 cup broccoli washed

DIRECTIONS:
1. Put the carrots, broccoli, and ginger through your Juice Extractor.
2. Pour juice in blender and add spirulina powder.
3. Blend for 1 minute. Have as is or chill and drink.

Cereals, Granola, Oatmeal, Porridge, Puddings

23 Recipes

OATMEAL MANGO and COCONUT DELIGHT

INGREDIENTS:
- 2 Tbsps. grated coconut
- 1 serving quick-cooking or rolled oats
- 1 Tbsp. raw honey or maple syrup or molasses
- ½ cup mango chopped
- 2 Tbsps. cashews chopped
- 2 Brazil nuts chopped
- 1 Tbsp. grounded flax seeds

DIRECTIONS:
1. Preheat oven to 350° F.
2. Spread the coconut on a rimmed baking sheet and toast, tossing occasionally, until golden for 3 to 5 minutes.
3. Prepare the oats in a pot which you will boil in a cup of water for 5 minutes. (*Remember that we believe in baking a large batch of oats for one hour in your oven to get rid of phytic acid, then keep it in jars to do your quick and easy recipes daily*).
4. Stir in the maple syrup, honey, or molasses.
5. Top with the mangoes, cashews, grounded flax seeds and the coconut.

NUTTY BANANA GRANOLA

INGREDIENTS:
- 2 medium sized ripe bananas
- ¼ cup pecans
- ¼ cup almonds chopped
- ¼ cup walnuts
- 6 large dates pitted
- ¼ tsp sea salt
- 2 ½ cups rolled oats
- ¼ cup shredded coconut
- ¼ cup organic raisins and dried cranberries (*optional*)
- 1 cup water or almond or rice milk

DIRECTIONS:
1. Preheat oven to 300°F. Line large baking sheet with parchment paper or use a non-stick stainless–steel pan.
2. Combine oats, coconut, almonds, pecans, walnuts, seeds (*pumpkin, sesame, sunflower*) in a large bowl. (*Any variety of nuts can be used instead e.g., cashew nuts, Brazil nuts*). NB. *Nuts will be added later on at 10 minutes before you turn the oven off.*
3. Combine salt, dates and water in a small saucepan and bring to a boil over medium heat for 5 minutes.
4. Remove from heat and cool. Pour into a blender and blend with bananas until smooth.
5. Pour this mixture over the dry ingredients and stir to coat. Spread mixture out evenly on baking sheet.
6. Bake in the preheated oven until crispy and toasted, about 1 hour. Stir every 20 minutes.
7. Cool, and then stir in the organic raisins and cranberries before storing in an airtight container.

OATMEAL with BANANA and MOLASSES

INGREDIENTS:
- 1 serving quick–cooking or rolled oats
- ½ banana sliced
- 2 Tbsps. pecans chopped and toasted
- 2 Tbsps. almond or organic soy milk
- 1 Tbsp. molasses

DIRECTIONS:
1. Prepare oats in a pot which you will boil in a cup of water for 5 minutes.
2. Top with banana and pecans. Drizzle with nut milk and molasses.

BANANA NUT GRANOLA

INGREDIENTS:
- 2 medium sized ripe bananas
- ¼ cup pecans
- ¼ cup almonds chopped
- ¼ cup walnuts
- 6 large dates pitted
- ¼ tsp. sea salt
- 2 ½ cups rolled oats
- ½ cup shredded coconut
- ¼ cup organic raisins and dried cranberries
- 1 cup water or almond or rice milk
- ¼ cup combined: pumpkin or sunflower and sesame seeds

DIRECTIONS:
1. Preheat oven to 300°F. Line large baking sheet with parchment paper or use non-stick stainless-steel pan.
2. Combine pumpkin seeds, sesame seeds, coconut, sunflower seeds, almonds, pecans, and walnuts in large bowl. *If there are other nuts prepared use them instead – e.g., Cashew nuts, Brazil nuts*
3. Combine in small saucepan salt, dates and water.
4. Bring to a boil over medium heat for 5 minutes then remove from heat and cool.
5. Pour in a blender and blend with bananas until smooth.
6. Pour mixture over dry oats and stir to coat. Spread mixture out evenly on baking sheets.
7. Bake coated oats in preheated oven until crispy and toasted for about 1 hour. Stir every 20 minutes.
8. At the end of 1 hour add in the pumpkin or sesame or sunflower seeds, nuts and shredded coconut and let bake for an additional 30 minutes.
9. Cool and then stir in organic raisins and cranberries before storing in an airtight container.

Have granola as is, or add a small amount of homemade almond or cashew or seed (*sunflower seeds, sesame seeds*) milk and enjoy with fruits of your choice!

FRUITS and NUTS BREAKFAST

INGREDIENTS:
- 1 ripe banana
- 1 ripe medium papaya
- ¼ cup roasted rolled oats
- 1 Tbsp. organic raisins
- 1 Tbsp. goji berries
- 1 Tbsp. sunflower seeds
- 6 prunes cut into smaller pieces
- 10 almonds sliced

DIRECTIONS:
1. Place roasted oats in a bowl. Then sprinkle nuts and dried fruits on top.
2. Pour ½ cup of homemade almond milk in bowl. Serve with banana and papaya.

PUMPKIN MILLET PORRIDGE

INGREDIENTS:
- pinch of sea salt
- 1 cup dry millet
- 1 cup pumpkin (*diced and cooked for 15 minutes*)
- 2 tsps. raw honey
- 1 tsp. ground coriander powder
- 1 tsp. pumpkin pie spice
- 1 cup coconut milk
- 1 tsp molasses or maple syrup

DIRECTIONS:
1. Soak your millet overnight in a pot of water. (*In the morning place the pot on the stove to boil and salt to taste*).
2. Stir in diced pumpkin (*reduce heat to low maintaining simmer*).
3. Cover and cook for about 25 minutes stirring occasionally. (*Once water is absorbed, turn off heat*).
4. With a fork, mash pumpkin, until it is smooth and combined with millet.
5. Stir in honey, coriander powder, coconut milk, spices, and molasses or maple syrup (*If porridge is thicker than you would like, stir in a bit of water or more coconut milk*).

GREEN PLANTAIN PORRIDGE

INGREDIENTS:
- 1 large green plantain (*with skin as this will thicken the porridge without the need to add any oats flour or other flours*)
- 1 cup pure water
- 1 cup coconut milk
- ¼ tsp sea salt
- 2 cinnamon leaves
- ¼ tsp coriander powder (*optional*)
- Toppings: organic raisins, nuts, seeds, fruits, coconut flakes

DIRECTIONS:
1. Wash and slice green plantain in about 1-inch pieces. Place in blender with 1 cup water and blend until smooth.
2. Pour into pot on low heat and add cinnamon leaves. Once it starts to boil, keep stirring with a large spoon to prevent lumps.
3. Boil for 10–15 minutes then add coconut milk, salt and coriander powder.
4. (*This replaces cinnamon bark powder which we don't use in our general cooking because it lowers the blood glucose drastically. However, it is used if this porridge was being made for a diabetic*).
5. Boil for another 5–7 minutes, then turn off the stove and remove cinnamon leaves.
6. Sweeten to taste using honey or maple syrup. Serves 2.

RIPE BREADFRUIT, COCONUT and MILLET PORRIDGE

INGREDIENTS:
- 1 cup blended ripe breadfruit
- 1 cup blended soft coconut jelly
- 1 cup pure water
- ½ cup cooked millet grain
- 2 Tbsps. sesame seeds
- ½ tsp sea salt
- Dash of coriander and anise powder
- Handful of organic raisins, sliced almonds, currants, sunflower seeds

DIRECTIONS:
1. Place ripe breadfruit, sesame seeds and soft coconut jelly in the blender with one cup of water.
2. Blend until coconut becomes chunky, the ripe breadfruit will be creamy and smooth.
3. Pour content into a pot at low or medium heat on the stove.
4. Bring to a boil then add in the cooked millet grain and salt to taste. Let simmer for 5 minutes.
5. **To cook your millet:** ½ cup millet to 1 ½ cups water. Bring to a boil and simmer for 1 hour until grains are soft.
6. Add coriander and anise powder and stir until all is combined.
7. Top porridge with organic raisins, dried currants, sliced almonds and sunflower seeds. *Enjoy for breakfast or lunch.*

BUCKWHEAT COCONUT PORRIDGE

INGREDIENTS:
- 1 ½ cups raw buckwheat groats, soaked overnight, drained, and rinsed
- 1 cup homemade almond milk
- 1 cup pure water
- ¼ cup maple syrup
- ½ tsp coriander powder
- ¼ tsp cardamom
- 1 vanilla bean, seeds scraped out, or 1 tsp non-alcoholic vanilla extract
- 1 Tbsp. ground flax meal
- Pinch sea salt
- ¼ cup shredded coconut
- Topping: fruits, nuts, organic raisins, dates, pumpkin seeds, sunflower seeds.

DIRECTIONS:
1. Place buckwheat groats in food processor and pulse a few times to break down.
2. Pour almond milk, maple syrup, coriander, and sea salt, and process until mixture has a smooth consistency (*but with some texture remaining*).
3. Pour in pot at low heat and add water (*depending on how thick you want porridge, add more or less water*) and let simmer for 5 minutes.
4. Add coconut and adjust spices. Divide porridge into four bowls and serve, topped with fresh fruits of your choice, chopped nuts, dates, organic raisins, pumpkin seeds, sunflower seeds or sliced bananas.

RICH COCOUNT MILK OATS PORRIDGE

INGREDIENTS:
- 2 cups roasted rolled oats
- 3 cups thick coconut milk (*preferably fresh done*)
- 2 Tbsps. coconut (*palm*) sugar or raw honey to taste
- Pinch of sea salt
- Pinch of coriander powder
- Dried fruit and extra grated coconut or coconut cream to top

DIRECTONS:
1. In a saucepan add coconut milk and salt. Bring to a boil and reduce heat, then add oats. *Remember we are using oats that has already been roasted for 1 hour in oven to cook and get rid of phytic acid.*
2. Allow porridge to come to a boil, and then reduce heat to very low. Cook for 20 minutes, and then add coconut sugar or honey and coriander.
3. Serve topped with grated coconut, coconut cream or dried or fresh fruits of your choice.

ORANGE and ALMOND MILLET PORRIDGE

INGREDIENTS:
- ½ cup millet
- 1 ½ cups coconut milk
- 2 dates chopped
- ½ Tbsp. orange zest
- 2 Tbsps. almond meal
- Juice of one orange
- Chopped almonds and coconut to serve

DIRECTIONS:
1. Combine the coconut milk and dates in a saucepan over a medium heat and bring to a slow boil.
2. Add rinsed millet (*soaked from the night before*), almond meal with the orange zest and juice.
3. Reduce the heat to low, and leave to cook for around 25 minutes, stirring occasionally (*add coconut milk or water as needed*).
4. Once porridge is cooked (*it should be creamy and not crunchy or gritty*), serve topped with chopped almonds and shredded coconut.

ALMOND MILLET PORRIDGE

Optional: Soak millet for 7 hours and then toast for 20 minutes in a 300°F oven as it may not have been pre-washed giving a slight bitter aftertaste. This will give you a much creamier porridge. (*I suggest completing steps one and two below with a larger amount of millet ahead of time and store in a container in your fridge. That way you can take out a breakfast portion whenever you like*).

INGREDIENTS:
- 1 cup whole millet
- 2 cups water
- 2 cups unsweetened almond milk
- ¼ tsp coriander powder (*used instead of cinnamon*)
- dash of sea salt
- maple syrup or raw honey to taste
- sliced almonds, toasted pecans, or any nut of choice to taste

DIRECTIONS:
1. Soak and toast millet as recommended above.
2. Grind cooled millet in a vita-mix or high-speed blender.
3. Heat almond milk and water in a saucepan over medium-low heat. Add a dash of salt as it heats.
4. Once it becomes hot and steaming, near boiling, slowly pour in your ground millet while whisking constantly.
5. Reduce heat to low, and continue whisking, making sure nothing is sticking to the bottom.
6. After about five minutes, millet will begin to thicken. The moment it reaches the consistency of a thick pudding, take it off heat and pour it into two bowls. (*It's better to take it off heat sooner than later, as it will also continue to thicken once in your bowl*).
7. For more flavor, add a tablespoon of maple syrup or honey and a small handful of nuts on top, if desired.

COCONUT PECAN BREAD PUDDING

INGREDIENTS:
- 8 Tbsps. flax seed gel
- 1 cup pure water
- 1 cup almond milk
- 3 Tbsps. virgin coconut oil (*plus more for pan*)
- 1/3 cup coconut cream
- ½ cup raw honey or desired sweetener
- 3 Tbsps. coconut or spelt flour
- ½ tsp sea salt
- 1 ½ cups shredded dried coconut
- ¾ cup pecan pieces
- 5 cups day–old whole wheat or whole grain bread broken into pieces

Optional: Add, according to preference or what's available:
- 1 tsp – 2 tsps ground coriander
- ½ cup organic raisins
- ¼ cup sliced almonds or pecans
- ¼ cup dried cranberries
- ½ cup currants

DIRECTION:
1. Preheat oven to 350°F.
2. In a large mixing bowl add flax seed gel, water, almond milk, coconut oil, coconut cream, honey, coconut flour, and salt. Beat until well mixed.
3. Fold in 1 cup of the dried coconut (*reserving ½ cup*), fruits or nuts of your choice and the bread pieces.
4. Mix only enough to evenly distribute ingredients and ensure all the bread is moistened with the mixture.
5. Pour mixture into oiled baking pan or casserole dish.
6. Sprinkle remaining ½ cup coconut flakes (*add more nuts if desired*) over mixture.
7. Bake in preheated oven for 10 minutes.
8. Reduce oven temperature to 325°F and bake for another 35 minutes, or until the top springs back when lightly tapped. Enjoy plain or topped with your favorite cream or fruit topping.

CORNMEAL COCONUT CREAM PUDDING

INGREDIENTS:
- 3 cups organic cornmeal
- ½ cup spelt or millet flour
- 1½ tsps. ground coriander
- ¼ cup shredded coconut
- 1 tsp sea salt
- 2 cups coconut milk
- 1 cup pure water
- ¼ cup coconut oil
- 3 ripe bananas (*instead of sugar*) or honey
- ½ cup raisins

Topping:
- 1 cup coconut cream
- ¼ cup raw organic honey
- ½ tsp ground coriander

DIRECTIONS:
1. Preheat oven to 350°F. Grease a 10" stainless steel baking pan.
2. Combine cornmeal with flour, coriander, coconut and salt in a large bowl.
3. In a saucepan, heat milk and water. Add oil and then crushed ripe bananas and organic raisins.
4. Mix well until liquid is heated, but not boiling.
5. Add half of warm liquid into dry ingredients and mix well.
6. Add rest of warm liquid and mix well until you have a smooth batter.
7. Ensure batter is mixed very well so that there are no lumps (*this can also be done in food processor*).
8. Pour into prepared baking pan and bake for 15 minutes.
9. In a small bowl, combine all topping ingredients and mix well.
10. After 15 minutes in oven, use a wooden spoon and stir batter to evenly distribute organic raisins.
11. Pour topping over pudding and bake for another 45 minutes.

HEALTHFUL COOKING -Recipes for Optimum Health Dr. Debra Williams **Recipe Cook Book 2021**

EASY LOW-CARB ALMOND BREAKFAST CEREAL

This is one of the many uses for the almond meal you will have left over from the process of making almond milk.
Easy vegan cold cereal with almond milk made, and almond meal left over.

This can be eaten plain, or with dried fruits, other seeds and nuts, fresh fruit, or as you desire, to make this a convenient, nutrient-packed, high-protein, high-fiber, vegan, soy-free way to start the day.

STRAWBERRY CHIA SEED PUDDING

Chia seeds are among the richest plant-based sources of omega-3 fatty acids, with more per serving than salmon. When mixed with liquid, the fiber-packed seeds resemble tapioca pudding, but with many more nutritional benefits, including boosting energy, aiding digestion and stabilizing blood sugar.

INGREDIENTS:
For the pudding:
- 2 ½ cups almond milk unsweetened (*made fresh at home*)
- ½ cup strawberries fresh or frozen
- ½ tsp ground coriander
- 1 tsp coconut sugar
- ½ cup chia seeds

For the cashew cream:
- ¼ cup cashews
- ¼ cup strawberries (*or any berries you like*)
- 2 Tbsps. pure water
- ⅛ tsp coconut sugar or raw honey

DIRECTIONS:
1. Blend almond milk, strawberries, coriander, coconut and sugar together in blender on high until smooth.
2. Pour strawberry mixture over chia seeds and whisk thoroughly. Let rest for 5 minutes then stir again.
3. After 10 minutes, stir again. Cover and refrigerate at least 3 hours or overnight.
4. Soak cashews in water and refrigerate for at least 3 hours or overnight.

5. **To make cream:** blend berries in blender until you have a smooth puree.
6. Drain and rinse the soaked cashews and add to blender along with cold water.
7. Blend until cashews are liquefied and have a smooth texture. Add coconut sugar and blend until well combined. Before serving, give pudding a good stir and divide into 4 cups.
8. Top with cream and more cherries, sunflower or pumpkin seeds and nuts of your choice.

BANANA CHIA PUDDING

INGREDIENTS:
- 3 Tbsps. flaxseeds (*grind to powder*)
- 3 Tbsps. chia seeds (*grind to powder*)
- 1 cup homemade almond milk
- 1 large ripe banana cut in chunks
- 1 Tbsp. honey or maple syrup
- 1 tsp pure vanilla
- ¼ tsp coriander powder
- ¼ tsp sea salt

DIRECTIONS:
1. Put milk, banana, flaxseeds, chia seeds, honey, vanilla, coriander, and sea salt in blender.
2. Blend until smooth. Pour mixture into a bowl and refrigerate until thickened, at least 2 hours.
3. Spoon mixture into small bowls to serve. Top with your favorite fruits, organic raisins, and nuts.

AUNTY RUBY'S NO-SUGAR SWEET POTATO PUDDING

INGREDIENTS:
- 2 lbs. sweet potatoes grated
- ¼ lb. yam grated
- 1 small coco or dasheen grated
- ½ cup organic raisins
- 3 cups coconut milk (*2 small coconuts blended in 2 cups water with the trash*)
- ½ cup raw honey
- 1 tsp sea salt
- ¼ cup coconut oil
- 2 ripe bananas (*mashed or blended*)
- 1 small ripe plantain (*cut into small cubes*)
- ½ cup spelt flour (*Optional - for a firmer pudding*)

DIRECTIONS:
1. Preheat oven to 350°F.
2. In a bowl mix potato, coco, ripe bananas, ripe plantain, yam, and raisins.
3. In another bowl mix coconut milk and trash, honey, coconut oil and salt.
4. Pour milk mixture into potato mixture and mix with a broad wooden spoon (*or regular spoon*) until well combined.
5. Pour into a greased 9-inch pan. (*Now we only use stainless steel, ceramic or glass baking containers. If you have the aluminum baking pan, you can line it with parchment paper or use banana leaf*).
6. Rest mixture for about half hour.
7. Bake at 350°F about 1 to 1 ½ hours until center is set.

NO-BAKE AVOCADO, CAROB and SWEET POTATO PUDDING

INGREDIENTS:
- 2 medium cooked sweet potato
- 1 medium avocado
- 4–6 dates pitted and soaked
- 2 Tbsps. carob powder (*chocolate substitute*)
- ¼ cup water (*plus more for blending*)
- ⅛ tsp sea salt

DIRECTIONS:
1. Combine all the ingredients in the bowl of a food processor and pulse until mixed.
2. While machine is running, drizzle in more water until the pudding is 100% smooth and creamy.
3. Serve with toast, fruit or alone. Top pudding with shredded coconut or nuts if your desire.

DEBRA'S MILLET COCONUT PUDDING

INGREDIENTS:
- ¾ cup millet
- 4 ½ cups pure water
- ½ cup cashew nuts
- 2 Tbsps. coconut or almond milk
- 4 Tbsps. raw honey or maple syrup
- ½ tsp. lemon zest
- ¼ tsp. coriander powder
- 1 tsp. pure alcohol-free vanilla
- ¼ tsp. sea salt
- ½ cup grated coconut
- ½ cup chopped dates mixed with raisins and cranberries
- ¼ cup sliced almonds,
- 2 Tbsps. wheat germ
- 2 Tbsps. flax seeds

DIRECTIONS:
1. In a saucepan bring millet and 4 cups water to a boil and simmer for 5 minutes at low heat.
2. Pour water off and blend with cashew nuts, coconut or almond milk, raw honey or maple syrup, lemon zest, coriander powder, pure alcohol-free vanilla and sea salt. Blend until smooth.
3. Put mixture in a glass or stainless-steel baking dish. Add grated coconut, chopped dates mixed with raisins and cranberries. Bake in oven at 350°F for 1 hour and 20 minutes.
4. At 45 minutes into baking, check pudding and stir in sliced almonds, wheat germ, flax seeds and remaining ½ cup of water with a spoon, Place back in oven and finish baking for the next 35 minutes.
5. Allow to cool for a few minutes, then enjoy for a warm healthy breakfast. Can be served with fruits, sunflower or pumpkin seeds.

MANGO CHIA SEEDS BREAKFAST PUDDING

Toppings (optional and open for substitution): drizzle of almond butter, pineapple, mango, fresh mint leaves, etc.

INGREDIENTS:
- ½ cup diced fresh ripe mango
- 1 cup coconut milk
- 2 Tbsps. grated coconut
- 4 Tbsps. chia or flax seeds
- 1 Tbsp. lime juice
- 1 Tbsp. raw honey or maple syrup (optional)

DIRECTIONS:
1. Blend mango, coconut milk, and lime juice (*honey or maple syrup, if using*) until smooth.
2. Stir blended mix with chia seeds and grated coconut in a bowl.
3. Cover and place bowl in fridge for a few hours, preferably overnight, for chia seeds to absorb the liquid and expand.
4. When ready to eat, add toppings and dig in.

GRANDMA WENDY'S MIXED PUDDING DELIGHT

INGREDIENTS:
- 1 medium sweet potato peeled and diced
- 1 medium Irish potato peeled and diced
- 1 cup yellow yam diced
- 2 cups grated coconut
- 1 cup spelt or rye flour (*or oatmeal flour or cornmeal*)
- 1 Tbsp. grounded flaxseeds
- 1 tsp sea salt
- ½ tsp coriander powder
- ½ tsp cardamom powder
- ½ cup raw honey or maple syrup
- 2 Tbsps. black strap molasses
- ½ cup organic raisins
- 2 cups pure water

DIRECTIONS:
1. Using food processor or blender, blend water with sweet potato, Irish potato and yam.
2. Add coconut, honey, molasses, salt and flaxseed powder and blend. Pour mixture into bowl.
3. Add spices and organic raisins (*you can add other dried fruits like prunes and dates and remove the honey and molasses if you wish*).
4. Slowly add flour, *quarter cup at a time*, as a large spoon is used to combine mixture.
5. Keep adding until all the flour is incorporated (*you may need to add a bit more flour at this point depending on how dry or moist you wish your pudding to be*) and you should have a nice pudding batter consistency.
6. Pour mixture into a baking dish and bake at 320°F for 1 hour.

CAROB-PEPPERMINT ZUCCHINI FUDGE

INGREDIENTS:
- ½ cup raw almonds
- 1 ⅓ cups strong hot peppermint herb tea
- 1 Tbsp. raw honey or maple syrup
- 1 cup raw unsweetened carob powder
- 1 cup grated zucchini
- ½ cup arrowroot powder
- ½ cup raw walnuts or pecan nut chopped

DIRECTIONS:
1. Grind almonds or walnuts to meal in a blender.
2. If tea has cooled down during steeping process, warm it up again so that it will activate the arrowroot powder. Stir honey into tea when it is finished steeping
3. Combine all ingredients well in large bowl.
4. Press into an 8 x 8 stainless steel cake pan or glass baking dish.
5. Bake in oven at 300°F for 20 minutes. Cool, chill and serve (*nicer when chilled*) or eat warm.

Pies

5 Recipes

CAROB BANANA ALMOND PIE

This is a favorite for children, so let them have fun in the kitchen helping you to make it.

CRUST:
- 1 cup almonds (*soaked overnight*)
- 6 dates
- 2 tsps. raw carob nibs or powder

CRUST DIRECTIONS:
1. Process ingredients together in a food processor until crumbly and the mixture sticks together.
2. Press into the bottom of a 9-inch pie plate or use six 8oz mini-plastic containers for ease of serving.

FILLING:
- 2 cups cashew (*soaked overnight*)
- 3 tsps. raw agave sweetener or honey or maple syrup
- 3 tsps. carob powder
- ⅛ tsp sea salt
- 2 Tbsps. cold pressed coconut oil
- 2 large bananas sliced into rounds

STRAWBERRY TOPPING:
- ½ cup of frozen or fresh strawberries
- 2 tsps. agave sweetener or maple syrup or honey

STRAWBERRY TOPPING DIRECTIONS:
1. Blend the ingredients together until nice and smooth.

PIE DIRECTIONS:
1. Combine all ingredients, except bananas, in a food processor until smooth. (*Mixture will be thick*).
2. Spread ½ the filling over pie crust.
3. Arrange banana slices evenly on top.
4. Spread remaining filling over bananas.
5. Top pie with sliced bananas and then cover with strawberry topping. Refrigerate until chilled and enjoy.

PUMPKIN-RIPE BANANA PIE

ALMOND CAROB CRUST:
- 1 cup raw almond soaked
- 3–4 dates or 2–3 Tbsps. maple syrup
- 3 Tbsps. carob powder
- 2 Tbsps. sesame seeds
- 2 Tbsps. Hemp seeds (*optional*)
- Pinch sea salt

DIRECTIONS:
1. Place all ingredients into a food processor or blender and pulse until combined.
 (*You want the crust to slightly stick together*).
2. Scoop almond carob crust into mini pie pans.
3. Press down with fingers to firmly place the crust into pan.
4. Set aside as you make your filling.

PUMPKIN–BANANA FILLING:
- 2 cups raw pumpkin diced
- 3 ripe bananas
- 3 Tbsps. cold pressed coconut oil
- ¼ cup maple syrup or agave nectar
- Dash of coriander and cardamom

DIRECTIONS:
1. Wash, peel, and cut the pumpkin into small pieces.
2. Peel the bananas and place into food processor or blender with maple syrup, spices, and oil.
3. Blend for a little bit to get it creamy and smooth.
4. Once pumpkin–banana filling is blended begin scooping your filling into your mini pie containers.
5. Fill them to the top and then top with some fresh ripe banana slices.
6. Set the pie in your refrigerator for an hour to chill.

SWEET POTATO SHEPHERD'S PIE

INGREDIENTS:
- 1 onion chopped
- 2 large carrots diced
- 3 celery stalks diced
- 2 cloves garlic minced
- 1 small tomato diced
- ½ tsp basil
- ½ tsp oregano
- ¼ tsp cumin
- ¼ tsp coriander
- 3 bay leaves
- ¼ tsp sage
- 2 Tbsps. molasses
- 2 cups cooked lentils
- ½ cup coconut milk or pure water
- 2 Tbsps. coconut oil
- ½ tsp sea salt
- Dash of cayenne pepper

TOPPING AND BOTTOM LAYER FOR THE PIE:
1. Peel and boil 3 large, sweet potatoes. Grater two cups of raw pumpkin.
2. In a food processor, mash the sweet potato and add 1 cup of the raw pumpkin to it. It should be creamy.
   (*You may need to add a little water to the food processor to get the potato very creamy*).

To cook the Lentil filling:
a) Heat coconut oil in a pan. Add carrot, celery, sweet pepper, onions, scallion, and minced garlic.
b) Let herbs and spices roast in oil for about 30 seconds. Then pour in coconut milk.
c) Allow this to come to a boil for a few minutes.
d) Add in cooked Lentils, sage, cumin, bay leaves, oregano, cumin, coriander, and salt.
e) Let this simmer for about 15 minutes or until liquid is reduced.
f) You may adjust sauce consistency by adding one tablespoon of arrowroot powder to thicken it.
g) Add molasses, cayenne, and salt last.

h) Leave to simmer for another 15 minutes. Give everything a good stir and turn off heat.

3. Grease bottom of baking dish with a small amount of coconut oil.
4. Take half the mashed potato and pumpkin and layer bottom of dish, add a layer of cooked lentil.
5. Cover lentils with remaining raw grated pumpkin and the remaining mashed potato.
6. Bake in an oven at 350°F for 30 minutes.

BREADFRUIT NUT PIE

INGREDIENTS:
- 1 ½ cups breadfruit partially ripe (*almost ripe*)
- 2 ripe bananas
- ¼ cup macadamia or almond nuts chopped
- 4 dates, seeded and chopped
- 2 tsp arrow root powder
- 4 Tbsps. shredded coconut
- 3 Tbsps. pure water or coconut milk
- ¼ tsp coriander powder
- 2 Tbsps. grounded flax and sunflower seeds
- ¼ tsp sea salt

DIRECTIONS:
1. Heat the oven to 350°F.
2. Mix and mash all ingredients in a mixing bowl or process in a food processor until smooth.
3. Lightly oil a stainless-steel bread pan or a glass bread baking dish.
4. Pour mixture into bread pan and bake for 30–35 minutes.

ZUCCHINI LIME (unbaked) COCONUT PIE

INGREDIENTS:
Crust:
- 1 cup medjool pitted dates
- ½ cup whole almonds
- ½ cup whole pecans
- ¼ cup shredded dried coconut
- Pinch of sea salt

Filling:
- 2 cups cashews
- 1 medium zucchini
- ½ cup fresh lime juice + zest
- ½ cup maple syrup or honey
- 4 Tbsps. virgin cold pressed coconut oil
- 1 Tbsp. chia or flax seeds grounded

DIRECTIONS:
1. Put all crust ingredients into food processor and process until ingredients stick together. Scrape down the sides as needed. Be sure to put parchment paper before pressing crust mixture into your square dish. This will help when it's time to cut.
2. Place all filling ingredients in your high-speed blender and blend until filling is completely smooth and creamy.
3. Pour filling evenly over pie crust and smooth with a spatula. Sprinkle your lemon zest on top and place in freezer to set for at least 2 hours.
4. Use large knife to cut into 3" bars and store in fridge until ready to eat. Enjoy!

Breads, Bun, Muffins, Pancake, Crackers

39 Recipes

WALNUT FLAT BREAD

INGREDIENTS:
- 1 1/3 cup oat bran
- ¼ cup walnuts
- 2 Tbsps. ground sesame seeds
- ¼ tsp sea salt
- ½ cup water
- 2 Tbsps. grounded flax seed powder

DIRECTIONS:
1. Place all ingredients into a food processor. Add the dried items first and then the liquid.
   (*If you don't have a food processor, use a blender*).
2. Process until all ingredients are combined. Flatten with rolling pin over parchment paper.
3. Bake at 300°F for 30 minutes.

VEGETABLE LENTILS FLATBREAD

INGREDIENTS:
- 1 cup sweet potato strips
- ½ cup Zucchini strips
- 4 scallion stalks chopped
- ¼ cup sliced bell pepper (*red or yellow*)
- 1 small onion sliced thinly
- 1 tsp. Himalayan Sea salt
- Herbs of your choice
- ¾ cup Oats or Spelt flour
- 1 cup water
- ½ cup Red Lentils

DIRECTIONS:
1. In a bowl, place potato strips, zucchini strips, scallion, bell pepper, onion, salt and herbs.

2. Pour water, flour and red lentils into a blender and blend until well combined.
3. Pour mixture into bowl with vegetables and coat well using a spoon.
4. Pour vegetable mixture on baking sheet covered with parchment paper (*or greased stainless steel or glass baking flat dish*). Bake at 325°F for 40 minutes.

RIPE BREADFRUIT FLAT BREAD

INGREDIENTS:
- ½ cup crushed ripe breadfruit
- ½ cup spelt flour
- ½ cup oatmeal flour
- 4 Tbsps. coconut milk
- Dash of sea salt
- 4Tbsps. virgin coconut oil

DIRECTIONS:
1. In bowl, pour in flour and salt. Add crushed ripe breadfruit and use fingers to combine.
2. Add coconut milk and oil. Knead into a nice dough, flatten out with your hand on pastry board.
3. Bake flat bread for 30 minutes at 350°F or on stove top in stainless steel pan with a cover for 15 minutes on each side.

BREADFRUIT and PLANTAIN FLAT BREAD

INGREDIENTS:
- 1 cup grated breadfruit (*can use slightly ripe breadfruit or left-over roasted breadfruit*)
- ¼ cup coconut milk
- ¼ tsp sea salt
- Herbs: basil, sage, garlic powder, parsley
- ¼ cup grated ripe plantain
- ½ cup oven dry cooked spelt flour
- 1 tsp turmeric powder
- 2 Tbsps. virgin coconut oil

DIRECTIONS:
1. Put all dry ingredients in bowl and combine them.
2. Add coconut oil, and then coconut milk slowly, until mixture can be combined and made into dough.
3. Break off handful pieces and roll out to a flatten bread about ½ inch thick (*can use rolling pin or your hand to flatten out dough*).
4. Place on heated skillet on stove and cook for 10 minutes on each side or place flat breads on baking sheet and bake in oven at 300°F for 25–30 minutes.

OATMEAL BUCKWHEAT FLAT BREAD

INGREDIENTS:
- 1 cup oats flour
- 1 cup shredded coconut
- 1 cup water or nut milk
- ¼ tsp. salt
- ½ cup buckwheat flour
- ¼ cup organic raisins
- ½ tsp coriander powder
- 1 Tbsp. ground flaxseeds
- 1 Tbsp. ground chia seeds
- 1 Tbsp. honey
- 2 Tbsps. coconut oil

DIRECTIONS:
1. Grind rolled oats in blender until it becomes the consistency of flour.
2. Pour into mixing bowl and add buckwheat flour, then add coconut, salt, and all other dry ingredients.
3. Add coconut oil, water or nut milk and stir to combine.
4. Bake in glass or stainless-steel bread dish or on flat baking sheet.
5. Place on parchment paper and extend with rolling pin. Bake at 300°F for 1 hour.

BARLEY COCONUT FLAT BREAD

INGREDIENTS:
- 4 cups barley flakes
- 1 cup shredded coconut
- 1 cup almond or coconut milk or water
- ½ tsp sea salt
- ½ cup spelt flour

DIRECTIONS:
1. Grind barley flakes in blender.
2. Add spelt flour, coconut, and salt. Mix it with water or milk.
3. Place on parchment paper. Extend with rolling pin. Bake at 300°F for 40 minutes.

GREEN PLANTAIN FLAT BREAD

INGREDIENTS:
- 1 medium green plantain
- 2 Tbsps. flaxseed meal (*grind the flaxseed to a powder*)
- ¼ tsp Himalayan or Celtic Sea salt
- 2 Tbsps. coconut oil
- Dash of onion powder and garlic powder (*optional*)
- ½ cup water

DIRECTIONS:
1. Peel skin off green plantain and cut into chuck sized pieces.
2. Place plantain in blender with other ingredients.
3. Blend until smooth, and then pour out on a flat baking sheet. Using a flat knife or a scapular to evenly lay it out about ½ inch in thickness.
4. Bake in an oven at 350°F for 30 minutes.

OATS FLAT BREAD

INGREDIENTS:
- 1 cup warm water
- 1 ½ cups roasted rolled oats
- 2 Tbsps. Raw honey
- ½ tsp. sea salt
- ½ tsp. turmeric powder
- Dash of garlic and onion powder (*optional*)
- 2 Tbsps. Flaxseed
- 2 Tbsps. Pumpkin seeds
- 2 Tbsps. Sunflower seeds
- 2 Tbsps. Chia seeds
- 2 Tbsps. Sesame seeds
- 3 Tbsps. Coconut oil

DIRECTIONS:
1. Pour dry oats in blender or food processor and blend until it becomes oats flour.
2. Grind all seeds into powder and add to oats in a bowl.
3. Add all other dry ingredients, then add water and coconut oil, using a spoon to combine all ingredients until you have a dough, then using your cleanly washed hands to form the dough neatly. Heat oven to 350°F. Using a rolling pin or your hands and flatten dough to 1 inch thick.
4. Place on baking sheet and bake for 30 minutes.

SWEET POTATO BEAN OATMEAL FLAT BREAD

INGREDIENTS:
- 1 cup cooked beans (*with sage, basil, oregano*)
- 1 cup cooked sweet potatoes
- 1 cup pure water
- 2 cups quick oats soaked for 4 hours
- ½ tsp sea salt
- 2 Tbsps. arrowroot powder

DIRECTIONS:
1. In a food processor or blender, mix or blend all ingredients.
2. Add the dried ingredients first then add liquid.
3. Pour out on parchment paper over cookie sheet.
4. Smooth out and shape with the dull edge of a knife or use your rolling pin (*make them circular or square*).
5. Bake at 300°F for 1 hour.

FLAXSEED FLAT BREAD

INGREDIENTS:
- 2 cups flax seed meal (*ground the whole flaxseed in your food processor or blender*)
- 2 Tbsps. arrowroot powder
- 1 tsp sea salt
- 1 cup Millet or Spelt flour
- 2 Tbsps. molasses
- ½ cup warm water or coconut milk
- 1/3 cup virgin coconut oil
- 2 Tbsps. raw honey

DIRECTIONS:
1. Preheat oven to 350°F. Prepare pan (*10 x 15 with sides' works best*) with parchment paper.
2. Mix dry ingredients very well. If you wish you can add organic raisins to recipe. (*Get creative and personalize recipe to your own taste. You can add grated coconut, nuts, etc.*).
3. Add wet ingredients to dry mixture and mix thoroughly. Let stand for a couple of minutes for mixture to thicken.
4. Pour batter onto pan. It is going to mound in the middle, so you will get a more even thickness if you spread it away from the center somewhat, in roughly a rectangle an inch or two from the sides of the pan.
5. Bake for about 35 minutes, until it springs back when you touch the top and/or is visibly browner than flax already is.
6. Cool, cut into whatever sizes you want, eat and enjoy!

TOMATO CHICKPEAS FLAX and CHIA FLATBREAD

INGREDIENTS:
- ½ cup chickpeas flour
- 2 medium ripe tomatoes chopped
- 1 small cucumber, chopped
- 3–4 Tbsps. chia seeds powder (*grind to powder in a blender*)
- 3–4 Tbsps. flaxseeds (*grind to powder in a blender*)
- ½ tsp. sea salt
- 2 stalks scallion
- ½ small onion chopped
- 1 clove garlic
- ¼ tsp fresh thyme leaves
- 1 tsp. coconut oil
- Herbs: basil, turmeric, parsley, sage, cumin

TOMATO-CHICKPEAS-FLAX AND CHIA FLATBREAD. SERVED WITH steamed OKRA, CHERRY-TOMATOES, STRING BEAN AND LIMA BEANS STEW....from Dr. Debs kitchen

DIRECTIONS:
1. In food processor or blender, blend cucumber, tomatoes, scallion, onion, garlic, and thyme leaves until well mixed.
2. In a bowl add chickpeas flour, salt, turmeric powder, coconut oil and all other herbs, mixing with a spoon until well incorporated. Pour wet ingredients from blender into bowl slowly, mixing as you go along.
3. Roll dough out onto a sheet of parchment paper and cut it into rectangles (*yields five (5) sizeable flatbreads*).
4. Turn on dehydrator and set to 118°F. Put bread onto a parchment paper-lined dehydrator tray, and place bread in machine. Dehydrate for about one hour, and flip bread. Dehydrate for another six hours or until bread has reached a consistency you like. (*Leave overnight in dehydrator, to have a warm, firm and sturdy texture flat bread the next morning ready for breakfast*).
5. If you don't have a dehydrator, bake this flat bread at 200°F for 30 minutes. Flip and finish baking for another 20–30 minutes.

BANANA APPLE NUT BREAD

INGREDIENTS:
- 3 ripe bananas
- 1 apple peeled and diced
- ½ cup raw honey or maple syrup
- 1 ¾ cups spelt flour
- ½ cup applesauce (*make your own: blend 1 apple with ¼ cup water in a blender until smooth*)
- 2 Tbsps. grounded flax seed
- ½ cup roasted oats
- 1 tsp sea salt
- 1 tsp coriander powder
- 2 Tbsps. chopped walnuts or almonds
- ¼ cup coconut milk
- 2 Tbsps. arrowroot powder

DIRECTIONS:
1. Preheat oven to 350°F. Lightly spray a 9–inch loaf pan. In a medium–sized bowl, mash the bananas with a fork.
2. Add the apple, honey, flour, applesauce, coconut milk, arrowroot powder, flax seeds, salt, and coriander to the bowl or use a food processor and mix well. (*If a food processor is used add the apple last when you are about to pour mixture into the baking pan*).
3. Pour into greased stainless–steel pan, and sprinkle with chopped walnuts.
4. Bake for 35 to 40 minutes or until a toothpick inserted in the middle comes out dry.
5. Cool in pan for 15 minutes, and then transfer to a cooling rack. (*If you don't have stainless steel baking pans, you can line your regular baking pans with parchment paper*).

BANANA NUT BREAD

INGREDIENTS:
- 6 small ripe bananas
- 4 Tbsps. organic raisins
- 1 Tbsp. black strapped molasses
- ½ tsp. sea salt
- 1 cup rolled oats (*already slow cooked or roasted for 1 hour*)
- ½ cup walnuts or almonds
- ½ shredded coconut
- ¼ cup sunflower seeds
- 1 cup almond or rice milk (*home-made coconut milk or water*)
- 1 cup spelt flour
- 3 Tbsps. flax seed gel (*egg replacer*)
- ½ tsp coriander powder

DIRECTIONS:
1. In food processor or powerful blender, mix bananas, salt, coriander, walnuts, oats, spelt flour, shredded coconut and salt until nuts and oats are all in small pieces.
2. Add in almond milk slowly and blend until well combined. Fill two (2) oiled baking dish ⅔ full.
3. Bake for 30–35 minutes at 325°F. Remove from oven and allow to cool in baking dish.
4. Remove from baking dish and slice in ½ inch slices for breakfast or lunch, served with fruits.
5. Store second bread in fridge, until you are ready to eat that one…enjoy!!

WALNUT (YEAST FREE) BREAD

INGREDIENTS:
- 1 cup pure water*
- 2 Tbsps. lecithin granules*
- 1 cup walnuts**
- 1 cup warm water**
- ½ cup grounded flaxseeds
- 1 tsp sea salt
- ¼ cup raw honey or other sweetener of choice
- 4 cups sifted whole wheat or spelt flour (*use any whole grain flour*)
- 2 Tbsps. arrow root powder

***Lecithin water mixture:** Blend water and lecithin granules until smooth.
****Walnut Butter:** Blend walnuts with warm water until smooth.

DIRECTIONS:
1. Place lecithin water mixture, walnut butter, flaxseeds, sea salt, honey into a larger bowl.
2. Add flour one cup at a time and arrow root powder mixing well until dough is no longer sticky.
3. Knead briefly and allow dough to sit for one hour covered in a warm place.
4. Punch down dough, shape into desired shape and place into a baking bread pan.
5. Bake in a pre–heated oven at 350°F for 30–35 minutes.

VEGETARIAN PUMPKIN WALNUT BREAD

INGREDIENTS:
- 3 Tbsps. flaxseed powder
- 2 cups pumpkin puree
- 1 cup pure water
- ½ cup grated coconut (*optional*)
- ¼ cup pumpkin seeds
- ⅓ cup maple syrup, coconut sugar or sub honey (*if not vegan*)
- 3 Tbsps. virgin coconut oil
- 2 Tbsps. arrowroot powder
- 1 tsp. ground coriander powder
- ½ tsp. cardamom powder
- 1 tsp sea salt
- 1 cup Spelt flour
- ⅓ cup oat flour
- ⅓ cup millet flour
- ¼ cup dried currants, cranberries, or cherries
- ¼ cup chopped walnuts

DIRECTIONS:
1. Preheat the oven to 325°F. Spray a 9X5-inch loaf dish with coconut oil.
2. In a large bowl, prepare flax by mixing hot water and flaxseed meal and let it rest for 5 minutes.
3. Add maple syrup, pumpkin puree, oil and stir.
4. Add arrowroot powder, spices, salt and whisk again. Then add water and whisk again.
5. Add oat, Millet, and Spelt flour, and stir until combined. If too thick, add a little more almond milk.
6. Add dried fruits or nuts, pumpkin seeds, and fold until incorporated. Fold in most of chopped walnuts, reserving some to sprinkle on top of batter once in the pan.
7. Pour batter into loaf pan and bake until top is browned, and a knife or toothpick inserted into center comes out clean, for about 50–60 minutes.
8. Allow to cool in pan for 10 minutes, then transfer bread to wire rack to cool completely before slicing.
9. Leftovers will keep fresh in airtight container or bag for several days.

MOLASSES SUNFLOWERSEED BREAD

INGREDIENTS:
- 2 cups Spelt flour
- ¼ cup molasses
- ½ cup raisins and black currant
- 1 cup water
- ¼ cup sunflower seeds
- 1 Tbsp. orange rind
- ½ teaspoon sea salt
- 2 Tbsps. chopped walnuts
- 1 Tbsp. psyllium husk powder
- 1 Tbsp. flaxseed powder
- 2 Tbsps. finely diced prunes
- 2 Tbsps. coconut oil

DIRECTIONS:
1. Mix all ingredients and pour into a greased Pyrex or stainless-steel baking pan.
2. Fill a baking pan with water (*about 3 cups*) and place on lower tray in the oven. Turn oven on to 350°F.
3. Place bread mixture on tray above water, so the steam can rise to provide moisture in oven for a softer moist bread. Bake for 1 hour. Cool and slice thinly.
4. Delicious when spread with homemade pineapple or strawberry jam. **Enjoy for breakfast with fruits**.

DEHYDRATED BANANA NUT BREAD

A soft dehydrated optimum health banana bread made with whole grains and nuts.

INGREDIENTS:
- 2 cups rolled oats
- ½ cup Brazil nuts
- ½ cup almonds
- ½ cup flax seed
- 1 Tbsp. ground chia seeds
- 3 medium bananas
- ¼ cup agave, honey, or maple syrup
- Raisin paste: (*¼ cup organic raisins and 3 Tbsps. water blended until smooth*) or pitted dates
- 1 tsp. coriander powder
- ½ tsp. salt
- 3 Tbsps. virgin coconut oil
- ¼ cup water or almond milk

DIRECTIONS:
1. Process oats, Brazil and almond nuts, and flax seeds into flour either together or separately, depending on tool used.
2. Add all ingredients to mixing bowl, mash bananas, and lightly fold everything together. Add water slowly until fully incorporated.
3. Using a spatula or large spoon spread out mixture like a round pizza or square (*½ inch thick*) and put on dehydrator sheet or baking sheet. Place into dehydrator for processing. *An oven could be used but the results vary*.
4. Dehydrate at 115–120°F for 7–8 hours until crust forms on the outside. Once bread is firm enough, cut into slices. When done it should be soft and chewy with a slight crust on the outside.

ARTISAN BREAD

This easy no-knead artisan bread recipe only has 7 ingredients. It has a soft and fluffy inside and perfectly crunchy crust!

INGREDIENTS:
- 2 ½ cups water lukewarm (warm to *about 120 degrees*)
- 1 ½ tablespoons instant yeast
- 1 tablespoon honey or maple syrup
- 2 tablespoons coconut oil
- ½ tablespoon Himalayan Sea salt
- 6 ½ cups Spelt flour or organic Whole wheat flour
- 1 teaspoon sesame seeds (*to sprinkle on top of the dough*)

DIRECTIONS:
In a large bowl, dissolve yeast, honey, and warm water. Allow to sit for 6 to 8 minutes until water is foamy.

1. Add in the salt and coconut oil. Mix in flour a cupful at a time until it's all incorporated. Dough will be slightly wet.
2. Cover your dough with a damp towel and set it in a warm place to rise for about 3 hours, or until the dough has at least doubled in size.
3. Cover dough (*make sure it can still breathe, don't seal completely*) and place in fridge for 8 hours. It is great to do this overnight and bake next morning also.
4. Take 1/2 of the dough (*or 1/3 for a smaller loaf*) out of the bowl, it's very wet, so lightly flour your hands, and pull it into the shape of your loaf. Dust the top with flour and slash it with a sharp knife (*flour keeps your blade from sticking*) and leave it to rise for 30 to 40 minutes. Store the rest of the dough in the refrigerator (*will keep well for 10 days*) to make fresh bread

later in the week.
5. Preheat oven to 350 degrees Fahrenheit. Place your dough on baking sheet covered with parchment paper, use your knife to put a cross on top of the dough and sprinkle on the sesame seeds. Bake for 40 to 45 minutes.

NOTES

1. **The dough will be wet.** This is intended to be a wet dough, don't keep adding flour expecting a loaf to form. We call this a "free-form" loaf of bread. Because it's no-knead, it needs to be wet in order for the gluten to form properly.
2. **Flour your hands and work-surface.** Using well-floured hands and work-surface will help tremendously in keeping the dough from being too sticky. You don't want to go crazy with the flour, but a well-coated surface is helpful.
3. **Wait to slice into the bread.** Wait at least 20 minutes before slicing into your loaf. If you slice into a hot loaf, you'll end up with a gummy center that will seem under baked.

For a softer crust - If you're not a fan of the crispy crunchy crust, you can immediately brush your loaf with coconut oil when it comes out of the oven. This will soften the crust just a bit so it's not so crunchy.

QUINOA OATS RAISIN BREAD

INGREDIENTS:
- 1 cup Quinoa Flour (*blend Quinoa grain to make your own*)
- 1 cup Oats Flour
- ½ cup Spelt flour
- 1 cup Sunflower seed or coconut milk
- ½ tsp. Himalayan Sea salt
- 1 Tbsp. non-alcoholic vanilla
- ¼ – ½ cup organic raisins
- 3 Tbsps. coconut oil
- ½ tsp. coriander powder
- ¼ cup grounded Chia seeds
- ¼ cup grounded Flax seeds
- ¼ cup raw honey or maple syrup
- ¼ cup crushed almonds and pecans (*use any nuts*)

DIRECTIONS:
1. Mix all dry ingredients in a bowl, and then slowly add wet ingredients one at a time.
2. Mix together using a large spoon, until you have a soft formed dough (*you will not need to use your hands*).
3. Using a glass or stainless-steel baking dish, grease with coconut oil, pour mixture in using a spoon and allow the dough to sit for 10–15 minutes on counter top.
4. Bake for 45 minutes at 300°F, then turn oven up to 350°F and finish baking for another 15–20 minutes or until top is golden brown. **The ingredients listed above will make two 8 x 8 inches' bread.**

RIPE PLANTAIN RAISIN BREAD

INGREDIENTS:
- 1 large ripe plantain
- 1 Tbsp. pumpkin seeds
- 1 Tbsp. sunflower seeds
- 2 Tbsps. sesame seeds
- 2 Tbsps. grounded flaxseeds
- 3 Tbsps. organic raisins
- 2 Tbsps. coconut oil
- ¼ tsp sea salt
- ¼ tsp coriander powder
- ½ cup water or nut-milk
- 1 Tbsp. raw honey or maple syrup

DIRECTIONS:
1. Place all ingredients in blender and blend until chunky (*or smooth if you like a less chunky bread*).
2. Pour into greased baking dish (*glass or stainless steel*). Bake at 350°F for 25 minutes.
3. Remove from oven and slice into four or six pieces. Brush top of each slice with raw honey or maple syrup and place back in oven for 10 minutes. **Enjoy with fruits for breakfast or lunch.**
4. When bread becomes golden brown on the top, remove from oven and allow to cool.

BANANA TAHINI RAISIN BREAD

INGREDIENTS:
- 3 medium sized ripe bananas
- ½ cup organic raisins
- ½ cup shredded coconut
- 1 Tbsp. tahini (*roasted sesame seeds*)
- ½ tsp. coriander powder
- ½ tsp. sea salt
- 2 Tbsps. wheat germ powder
- 1 cup blended rolled oats
- ½ tsp. grated ginger
- 1 Tbsps. black strapped molasses
- 2 Tbsps. honey or maple syrup
- ½ cup barley or spelt flour
- ½ cup water
- 3 Tbsps. coconut oil
- 2 Tbsps. flaxseed meal
- 1 Tbsp. pumpkin seeds
- 1 Tbsp. sunflower seeds

DIRECTIONS:
1. Heat oven to 350°F. Blend or coarsely smash ripe bananas. In mixing bowl, combine bananas, organic raisins, oil, water, tahini, honey, molasses, shredded coconut, and salt. Mix with a fork to combine. Stir in remaining ingredients until fully combined. Let sit for 2–3 minutes on counter.
2. Pour mixture into greased baking dish (*can use a little coconut oil to grease baking dish*). Bake for 40 minutes until golden brown. *Serve with raisin and sunflower seed butter.*

RIPE PLANTAIN COCONUT CASHEW RAISIN BREAD

INGREDIENTS:
- 1 large ripe plantain
- ¼ cup grated coconut
- 3 Tbsps. raw cashew
- 1 Tbsp. chia seeds
- 1 Tbsp. pumpkin seeds
- 1 Tbsp. sunflower seeds
- 2 Tbsps. sesame seeds
- 2 Tbsps. grounded flaxseeds
- 3 Tbsps. organic raisins
- 2 Tbsps. coconut oil
- ¼ tsp sea salt
- ¼ tsp coriander powder
- ½ cup pure water
- ½ cup Spelt Flour

DIRECTIONS:
1. Place ingredients in blender or a food processor. Blend or mix until smooth. Pour into a greased baking dish. Bake at 350°F for 30 minutes

DR DEBS SWEET CORN COCONUT RAISIN BREAD

INGREDIENTS:
- 1 cup corn flour
- 1 cup durum semolina flour
- ½ cup spelt flour
- 3 Tbsps. arrowroot powder
- ¼ cup organic raisins
- 1 ½ cups warm water
- 2–3 Tbsps. raw honey or maple syrup
- ½ cup grated coconut
- 1 tsp. sea salt (*Celtic or Himalayan*)
- 1 tsp. coriander powder
- 5 Tbsps. flaxseed meal (*freshly grind*)
- 3 Tbsps. coconut oil

DIRECTIONS:
1. In large bowl, add warm water and flaxseed meal.
2. Add honey, coconut oil, grated coconut, salt, organic raisins and coriander powder.
3. Mix together, then add dry ingredients one at a time, folding each into mixture with large mixing spoon.
4. Let sit for 5 minutes. Bake at 350°F for 40 minutes to golden brown and then turn oven down to 200°F.
5. Allow to finish baking for another 15 minutes or until thoroughly done. Cool and serve.

FLAXSEED RAISIN BREAD

INGREDIENTS:
- ½ cup coconut oil + extra for greasing baking pan
- ¼ cups maple syrup or raw honey
- 3 cups spelt flour
- 1 cup Graham flour
- ½ cup warm water
- ½ tsp salt
- 2 Tbsps. arrowroot powder
- 4 Tbsps. flaxseed powder (*grind seeds in blender*)
- ¾ cup coconut milk with sunflower seeds (*make coconut milk first, then blend in ¼ cup sunflower seeds*)

DIRECTIONS:
1. Preheat oven to 325°F.
2. Using an electric mixer or a fork, beat coconut oil and honey or maple syrup together until combined.
3. Add flour, water, salt, organic raisins, and arrowroot powder to bowl.
4. Add coconut or sunflower seed milk slowly until batter is sticky. The dough will be semi-firm and sticky.
5. Transfer dough from bowl to greased 9x9 baking pan using a large spoon. Gently flatten dough in pan.
6. Bake for 1 hour or until edges of flax-raisin bread is browned, and you can test the inside by putting a knife through the middle, if it comes up dry, the middle is baked.
7. Let cool for several minutes before cutting into flax-raisin bread. This is an easy, simple recipe which will provide you with a warm and delicious addition to your breakfast, lunch, or dinner.

ALMOND FLOUR BANANA BREAD

This tender banana bread packs a punch of protein, fiber, vitamins and mineral... making it perfect for a quick breakfast or lunch option, to be consumed with fruits of your choice.

INGREDIENTS:
- 2 cups almond meal or almond flour
- 1 cup roasted oats flour
- 2 tsps. arrow root powder
- ½ tsp sea salt
- ¼ cup coconut oil
- ¼ cup + 3 Tbsps. freshly ground chia seeds
- ¾ cup water or nut milk
- 2 Tbsps. wheat germ
- 4–5 very ripe bananas (*add more for a softer bread*)
- 1 Tbsp. ground coriander
- ¼ cup honey or maple syrup
- Coconut oil for greasing baking dish or pan

DIRECTION:
To dry roast your oats – put 1 pack of rolled oats in the oven at 200°F for 1 hour and bake. Then pour amount needed in blender and blend until it becomes like flour.

1. Preheat oven to 350°F and grease a 9 x 5 glass or stainless-steel loaf pan well.
2. Using a coffee or spice grinder machine (*or a magic bullet mini power blender*), grind the ¼ cup chia seeds first, and then measure what you need for the recipe.
3. Mix ¼ cup of ground chia seeds with ¾ cup water and allow to sit in fridge for 5 minutes to achieve "chia eggs" gel. Remove from the fridge then mash in ripe bananas. (*To avoid chunky pieces of banana in the bread you can blend them out*).
4. Combine the rest of the ingredients in a medium bowl, add chilled chia eggs and bananas, and mix well until a batter is formed.
5. Transfer to the greased loaf pan and use a spatula to smooth the top.
6. Bake for 35–40 minutes, until golden brown and when a knife is inserted in center of loaf comes out clean.
7. Allow to cool in pan for 10 minutes, then transfer to a wire rack to cool completely. Slice and serve!

SWEET POTATO CORN BREAD

INGREDIENTS:
- 2 Tbsps. flaxseed gel (*thick and gooey like egg whites*)
- 2 cups coconut milk
- 3 Tbsps. coconut oil
- ½ cup raw honey or maple syrup
- 1 ½ cups whole wheat pastry or spelt flour
- 1 cup sweet potato grated
- 1 cup cornmeal or millet flour
- ¼ cup grounded sunflower seeds
- 2 Tbsps. arrow root powder
- 1 tsp sea salt
- ½ tsp coriander powder

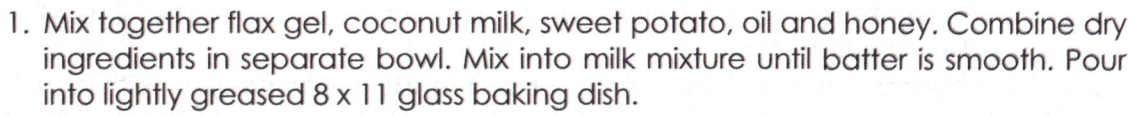

DIRECTIONS:
1. Mix together flax gel, coconut milk, sweet potato, oil and honey. Combine dry ingredients in separate bowl. Mix into milk mixture until batter is smooth. Pour into lightly greased 8 x 11 glass baking dish.
2. Bake in a 425°F oven for 35 minutes. (*In food processor, pour in dry ingredients, then add wet ingredients, pulse until smooth and then pour into baking dish*).

SWEET POTATO BUN

INGREDIENTS:
- ½ cup raw honey
- 2 Tbsps. molasses
- ½ cup of pure water or coconut milk
- 2 tsps. cumin powder
- 1 tsp. coriander powder
- 4 Tbsps. virgin coconut oil
- 4 Tbsps. grounded flax seeds (*to replace Egg*)
- 3 cups spelt flour
- 4 tsps. arrow root powder
- 1 ½ cups pureed Sweet Potato (*2 boiled sweet potatoes*)
- 1 cup organic raisins and cranberries mixed
- ½ tsp. sea salt

DIRECTIONS:
1. Preheat oven to 350°F. Grease standard loaf pan using cooking spray.
2. Line with parchment paper then spray again. Peel sweet potatoes, dice into 1-inch cubes to boil faster.
3. Add to boiling water and cook until soft and tender when pierced with knife for about 15 minutes or more. Strain off excess water. Puree sweet potato chunks in blender and measure 1 ½ cups for batter. Allow to cool.
4. In saucepan, add flaxseeds and coconut milk then warm at low heat then add honey, molasses, and spices.
5. Over low heat, stir but do not bring to a boil, then whisk in coconut oil until all is combined.
6. In medium bowl, add flour, salt and arrow root powder.
7. Gradually add wet mixture (*flaxseeds, coconut milk or water, honey, molasses and spices*), mixing well to combine. Stir in sweet potato puree, then fold in organic raisins and cranberries.
8. Pour into prepared loaf pan and bake for 45 minutes or until knife inserted comes out clean.
9. In a small pan, combine 1 tsp. coconut oil and honey. Brush over the bun when cooled.

STUFF CABBAGE LENTIL ROLLS

INGREDIENTS:
For the Sauce:
- 3 cups diced tomatoes
- 1 cup tomato paste
- 1 cup vegetable broth or water
- 1 Tbsp. coconut oil
- 1 small onion diced
- 3 cloves garlic minced
- 3 stalks scallion diced
- 1 Tbsp. raw honey or maple syrup
- ½ cup coconut cream
- ½ tsp. sea salt to taste

For the Rolls:
- 1 medium Cabbage
- 1 cup cooked lentils
- ½ cup cooked brown rice
- ¼ cup minced Onion sautéed
- Herbs: sage, parsley, basil, turmeric, and ginger to taste
- Salt and cayenne pepper to taste

DIRECTIONS:
FOR THE SAUCE:
1. In a large sauté pan, add coconut oil, garlic, scallion, and diced onions. Sauté until soft and translucent.
2. Add diced tomatoes and vegetable stock. Season with salt, herbs, and cayenne pepper.
3. Add tomato paste and taste again for seasoning. Add honey to balance out bitterness of herbs.
4. Bring to a boil then lower to a simmer for 20 minutes. Add coconut cream and simmer for another 10 minutes.

TO PREPARE THE CABBAGE LEAVES:
1. Partially boil head of cabbage just enough until you can gently peel away each layer, intact. *Cut core out of the whole head so the pieces can come off better*. Do not overcook. The leaves should be crisp still, but pliable.
2. Drain on a paper or kitchen towel. Repeat until the whole cabbage is done. Only use the biggest, best leaves.

FOR THE FILLING:
1. Mix together all ingredients for the rolls and add ½ cup of sauce mixture to help bind.
2. Place amount of mixture proportionate to the leaf in the center. Do not overfill.
3. Roll, tucking in the ends like an egg roll. *If necessary, you can use a toothpick to hold them together, but BE SURE to remove before serving!* Repeat with all cabbage leaves.
4. Place all finished rolls into a large sauce pot or a crock pot, stacking largest to smallest. Add all the sauce to cover. If needed, add some additional vegetable broth or water. Bring to a boil then lower to a simmer.
5. Cook for 10 minutes until sauce is bubbling, cabbage leaves are more translucent, and filling is hot inside.

RIPE BANANA RAISIN ROLLS

DON'T WASTE BANANAS   No Knead, No Eggs, No Sugar, No Milk! Super Soft and Heal

INGREDIENTS:
- 3 large very ripe bananas
- Active dry yeast 3g (*1 teaspoon*)
- ½ teaspoon Salt (*1.5g*)
- 1 tablespoon flaxseed meal (*replaces 1 egg*) Bread or unbleached all-purpose flour 35 0g (2 $1/3$ cups) - Spelt or organic whole wheat flour can be used also
- 2 tablespoons coconut oil
- ½ cup Raisins (*80g*)

DIRECTIONS:
1. Mash the ripe bananas in a bowl using a fork. Place the flax meal in a cup and add 6 tablespoons warm water, set aside for 5 minutes then pour into the bowl with the bananas. Next, add the dry yeast and mix with a spoon. Add the salt, coconut oil and raisins. Pour in the flour cup by cup, while mixing with a large spoon. Once the mixture comes together to form a dough, remove the spoon, and cover the bowl with a dry tablecloth. Let sit for 2 hours.
2. Sprinkle flour on the counter and take the dough out of the bowl and place on top. Using your hands flatten the dough, while folding to take out the bubbles. Form a round disk with the dough, then use a sharp knife to cut into 8 pieces. Roll each piece into a ball (dusting with flour if needed so it is not so sticky). Place the rolls on a baking sheet and place in a pre-heated oven at 300 degrees Fahrenheit. Bake for 35 to 40 minutes. After baking brush coconut oil or vegan butter over the tops so that the rolls remain soft.

BANANA BREAD BREAKFAST MUFFINS

INGREDIENTS:
- 6 small bananas
- ½ cup pecans
- 6 large dates pitted
- ¼ tsp salt
- 1 cup rolled oats toasted
- ½ cup walnuts
- ½ shredded coconut
- 1 cup almond or rice milk

DIRECTIONS:
1. (*Soak nuts for at least eight hours to reduce the amount of phytic acid*).
2. In a food processor or powerful blender mix bananas, walnuts, oats, pecans, dates, shredded coconut, and salt together until nuts and oats are reduced to small pieces.
3. Add almond milk slowly and blend until well combined.
4. Fill oiled muffin tins ⅔ full. Bake for 30–35 minutes at 300° F. Remove from pan to cool.
   Makes 12 muffins or 8 x 8 cake. (*Serve as a breakfast meal, after you have had your two servings of fresh fruit*).

CARROT CAROB PECAN NUT MUFFINS

INGREDIENTS:
- 2 large carrots washed and cleaned
- ½ cup raw honey
- 2 Tbsps. molasses
- 4 Tbsps. cold pressed coconut oil
- 1 Tbsp. soy lecithin
- 4 Tbsps. soy or almond milk
- 1 tsp grated orange zest
- ¼ cup carrot juice
- ¼ tsp sea salt
- ½ tsp coriander powder
- ⅔ cup carob powder
- 1 cup spelt or whole wheat flour
- ¼ cup pecan nuts
- ½ cup roasted rolled oat
- ½ cup shredded coconut
- 1 tsp flax seed and chi seeds grounded

DIRECTIONS:
1. Cut carrots into cubes and place in a food processer, then chop until fine.
2. Add all wet ingredients and then all other dry ingredients.
3. Use a scoop or tablespoon to remove mixture and place in stainless–steel muffin tin or parchment muffin cups. Sprinkle some crumbled pecans on top. Bake for 35–40 minutes at 350º F.

BANANA GINGER MUFFINS

INGREDIENTS:
- 3–4 ripe medium sized bananas mashed
- 1 Tbsp. grated fresh ginger
- 4 Tbsps. flax seed meal
- ¼ cup raw honey
- 2 Tbsps. blackstrap molasses
- 1 cup spelt flour
- ½ cup rolled oats
- 1 tsp. sea salt
- 4 Tbsps. virgin coconut oil
- 2 Tbsps. arrowroot powder
- ½ tsp. coriander powder
- ¼ cup pure water or coconut milk
- ¼ cup mixed seeds: pumpkin, sunflower and grounded sesame seeds
- ¼ cup shredded coconut

DIRECTIONS:
1. Preheat oven to 350°F. Grease stainless steel muffin baking sheet (*or parchment paper muffin baking cups*) with coconut oil. Mix bananas, water or nut milk, grated ginger, coconut oil, honey and molasses in large bowl. Whisk together flour, rolled oats, flax seed meal, arrowroot powder, shredded coconut, seeds, coriander and salt in medium bowl.
2. Add dry mixture to wet mixture and stir until combined. Pour batter into muffin cups.
3. Bake in preheated oven for 40 minutes or until wooden skewer comes out clean. Let cool and enjoy.

PECAN COCONUT PINEAPPLE MUFFINS

INGREDIENTS:
- 1 ½ cups fine shredded or flaked coconut
- ½ tsp. sea salt
- 1 cup pineapple chunks or blended pineapple
- ¼ cup roasted oats blended flour
- 3 Tbsps. honey or maple syrup
- 1 ½ tsp. finely grated lemon or lime peel zest
- Juice of 1 lemon or 2 small limes
- ¼ cup water or coconut milk
- 1 cup Durum Semolina flour
- ¼ cup chopped pecan nuts
- ½ tsp. grated ginger

DIRECTIONS:
1. In mixing bowl, combine blended pineapple or chunks, ginger, honey, oats flour and durum semolina flour. Mix in lemon or lime zest and juice, water or coconut milk, salt, coconut flakes and pecans.
2. Scoop into muffin cups using a tablespoon. Bake at 325°F in oven for 30–35 minutes until golden brown.
3. Drizzle a little honey or maple syrup on top of each muffin. Transfer to cooling rack. Cool completely. Enjoy alone or with your favorite fruits.

BUCKET WHEAT APPLE COCONUT MUFFINS

INGREDIENTS:
- 2 tsps. flaxseed freshly grounded
- 1 tsp chia seeds freshly ground
- 1 cup boiling water
- 1 cup room temperature water
- 1 cup buckwheat flour
- 1 cup spelt flour
- 1 Tbsp. arrowroot powder
- 2 Tbsps. wheat germ
- 1 Tbsp. lemon zest
- 2 Tbsps. lemon juice
- 2 medium granny apples sliced
- ½ tsp Celtic or Himalayan Sea salt
- 2 Tbsps. black strapped molasses
- ½ cup grated coconut flakes
- ½ tsp coriander powder
- Dash of Ceylon cinnamon powder
- 2 tsps. coconut sugar

DIRECTIONS:
1. Pre-heat oven at 325°F.
2. Put grounded chia and flaxseeds in bowl and pour on boiling water, let sit for 5 minutes until it becomes like gel. Set aside.
3. In a large bowl or food processor combine dry ingredients.
4. Put apples in blender with ¼ glass of water and blend until you have applesauce consistency.
5. Combine molasses, grated coconut, applesauce, ½ cup water and lemon juice and zest. Stir in chia or flaxseed gel.
6. Add wet ingredients to dry ingredients and mix thoroughly. Add salt, Ceylon cinnamon and coriander.
7. Grease muffin tin with coconut oil.
8. Add batter to ½ the height of each muffin pocket (*leave room for muffins to rise*).
9. Top with mixings of choice.

APPLE OATS MUFFINS

These dense, hearty muffins are a perfect component to a weekend breakfast spread - try pairing with sliced fruit.

INGREDIENTS:
- 2 cups yellow or green apples peeled and shredded
- 1 ½ cups all-purpose flour
- 1 cup roasted rolled oats
- ⅔ cup raw honey or maple syrup
- 1 ½ tsps. arrowroot powder
- 6 tsps. flaxseed gel
- ½ tsp sea salt
- ½ tsp ground coriander
- ¼ tsp ground cardamom
- ¼ cup almond nut milk
- 3 Tbsps. coconut oil
- ½ cup coconut jelly
- 2 Tbsps. lemon juice
- 1 tsp lemon zest
- 2 probiotic capsules (*open the casing and pour out the powder*)

DIRECTIONS:
1. Place shredded apple on paper towels and squeeze until barely moist; set aside. (*Note: a large-holed grater works just fine for shredding apple - no need to pull out your food processor.*)
2. Lightly spoon flour into dry measuring cups and level with a knife. Combine flour in a bowl with oats, honey, arrowroot powder, salt, cardamom and coriander. Make an opening in the center of mixture.
3. In another bowl, whisk together nut milk, coconut oil, lemon zest, coconut jelly (*blended until creamy*), lemon juice and probiotic powder. Add milk mixture to flour mixture, stirring until moist. Stir in apple.
4. Divide batter evenly among 12 muffin cups coated with cooking spray.
5. Bake at 350°F for 35–40 minutes, or until muffins spring back when touched in the center. Transfer immediately to wire rack to cool.

SAVORY CHICKPEA PANCAKE

This dense and filling savory chickpea pancake is packed with protein and fiber. Feel free to change up the mixture and toppings based on what you have in your refrigerator. To prevent it from sticking to the stainless steel skillet, be sure to spray the skillet liberally with olive oil before pouring on the batter. I also suggest chopping the veggies finely so they cook faster.

INGREDIENTS:
- 1 green onion finely chopped (*about ¼ cup*)
- ¼ cup red pepper finely chopped
- ½ cup chickpea flour
- ¼ tsp garlic powder
- 1 scallion stalk chopped
- ¼ tsp fine grain sea salt
- ¼ tsp grounded flax seed
- ½ cup distilled water
- Dash of dried herbs (*basil, cumin, sage*)
- For serving salsa, avocado, hummus, cashew cream (*optional*)

DIRECTIONS:
1. Prepare the vegetables and set aside. Preheat a 10-inch skillet over medium heat.
2. In a small bowl whisk together the chickpea flour, garlic powder, salt and flax seeds powder.
3. Add the water and whisk well until no clumps remain. (*Whisk for 15 seconds to create lots of air bubbles in the batter*).
4. Stir in chopped vegetables.
5. When the skillet is pre-heated (*a drop of water should sizzle on the pan*), spray it liberally with olive oil.
6. Pour in all batter (*if making 1 large pancake*) and quickly spread all over pan.
7. Cook for about 5–6 minutes on one side (*timing will depend on how hot your pan is*), until you can easily slide a pancake flipper or spatula under pancake and it's firm enough not to break when flipping.
8. Flip pancake carefully and cook for another 5 minutes, until lightly golden. Be sure to cook for enough time as this pancake takes much longer to cook compared to regular pancakes.

9. Serve on a large plate and top with your desired toppings.
10. Leftovers can be wrapped up and placed in fridge. Reheat on a skillet until warmed throughout.

CASHEW BANANA OATS WAFFLES

INGREDIENTS:
- 1/3 cup raw cashew nuts
- 1/3 cup pure water
- 2 ripe bananas
- 1 cup coconut or sunflower seed milk
- 2 Tbsps. wheat germ
- 1 tsp. pure vanilla
- 1 tbsp. virgin coconut oil
- 2 cups roasted rolled oats
- 2 Tbsps. flax seed powder

DIRECTIONS:
1. Blend cashew nuts and bananas in water and nut or seed milk until smooth in blender.
2. Add remaining ingredients, and blend. Let mixture stand 5 minutes to thicken.
3. Cook approximately 7 minutes in hot waffle iron until golden brown.
4. *If you don't have a waffle iron machine, pour mixture out into a stainless-steel frying pan and it will do nicely also.*
5. Cook on one side for 4 minutes, then flip and do other side for 4 minutes. You can get 3 to 4 waffles from this mixture. Serve hot with your favorite fruit or nut topping.

FLAX OATMEAL CRACKERS

INGREDIENTS:
- 1 ½ cups roasted rolled oats (*left whole or processed to desired consistency*)
- ½ cup corn meal or millet flour (*I prefer the millet flour, since it is a bit difficult to get non-GMO organic corn meal these days*)
- ½ cup flax seed grounded
- ½ cup spelt flour
- ½ tsp sea salt
- 1 Tbsp. arrowroot powder
- 2 Tbsps. coconut or olive oil
- ½ cup warm water (*you may need slightly less*)
- ½ cup raw honey

DIRECTIONS:
1. Mix oats, spelt flour, corn meal, flax seeds, salt and arrowroot powder.
2. Add oil and honey then mix well
3. Add enough water until dough comes together.
4. Roll dough to about ¼ centimeter thickness and cut into desired shapes. Prick with fork and mark off squares.
5. Bake at 300°F for about 45 minutes until crackers start turning brown.

CHICKPEAS and FLAX BISCUITS

INGREDIENTS:
- 1 cup chickpea flour (*if you have a powerful blender, you can grind 1 cup dried chickpea and make your own flour*)
- ½ tsp. sea salt (*Himalayan or Celtic*)
- Pinch of cumin powder
- 2 Tbsps. coconut oil
- 1 Tbsp. honey
- 3–4 Tbsps. flaxseed meal (*Grind the seeds to make your own*)
- Herbs: dill, sage, turmeric powder, parsley, garlic powder (*use herbs you like or not at all*)
- 3 Tbsps. sweet potato flour (*optional*)
- ½ cup water

Aunty Debs Chickpeas and Flax Biscuits

DIRECTIONS:
1. In a large mixing bowl add dry ingredients, and then wet ingredients one by one. Slowly add water as you mix with a spoon, forming a soft dough.
2. Remove spoon when mix is combined and use your clean hands to form a nice round dough. (*You may not use all of the water*). If dough is too wet, just add some more chickpeas flour or sweet potato flour.
3. Let sit for about 10 minutes, then break dough into three small pieces.
4. Using two layers of parchment paper, on a large flat cutting board or kitchen counter, place dough in the middle of one layer then place other layer on top of dough (*now dough is sandwiched by both layers*).
5. Using rolling pin, start flattening dough; rolling evenly until you have a nice flat biscuit thickness.
6. Tear off upper parchment paper, and then use a sharp knife to slice into 1–2 inch strips (*down first, then across*).
7. Put sliced dough (*do not remove from parchment paper*) on a baking sheet and place in oven.
8. Bake at 300°F for 20–25 minutes. When golden and crispy, turn off oven and allow to cool.

HEALTHFUL COOKING -Recipes for Optimum Health

Desserts:

Chips, Cookies, Bars, Balls

13 Recipes

KALE CHIPS

Kale has many health benefits, from weight management to healthy eyesight.

INGREDIENTS:
Basic chips:
- 2 Cups of kale washed and thoroughly dried
- 2 Tbsps. olive or coconut oil
- Sea salt for sprinkling

Zesty chips:
- Basic chips ingredients
- 1 Tbsp. lemon juice
- Dash of herbs and garlic powder

DIRECTIONS:
1. Preheat oven to 275°F. Remove ribs from kale and cut into 1 ½ inch pieces or just tear with your fingers. Spread on a baking sheet and toss with olive or coconut oil and salt.
2. (*For Zesty Cheesy Kale Chips add required ingredients listed above*). Massage all ingredients into kale.
3. Bake until crisp, turning leaves halfway through, about 20 to 30 minutes. Serve as finger food.
4. If using a dehydrator, then pop them in and they will be crisp in about 6 hours at 104°F. (*This method retains all nutritional value of kale, creating a low-calorie, nutrient-dense snack that is quite beneficial for your health*).

BANANA OATS COOKIES

INGREDIENTS:
- 2 cups rolled oats
- 1 cup spelt or whole wheat or quinoa or oats or barley flour
- ¼ cup sunflower seeds
- ¼ tsp sea salt
- 1 cup pureed overripe banana (*roughly 4 large bananas*)
- 4 Tbsps. raw honey
- 1 cup shredded coconut
- ½ cup organic raisins
- 6 prunes diced
- Hand full of pumpkin and sesame seeds
- 1 Tbsp. grounded flax seeds
- 1 Tbsp. black strap molasses
- 2 Tbsps. organic coconut oil

DIRECTIONS:
1. Preheat oven to 300°F. In a mixing bowl, combine rolled oats, flour, organic raisins, diced prunes, shredded coconut, sea salt and seeds. Use a large spoon to stir until well combined.
2. Add pureed banana, honey and coconut oil to dry mixture, and stir until combined. Using a cookie scoop or spoon, place mounds of batter (*about 2 tablespoons*) on a baking sheet lined with parchment paper.
3. Bake for 45 minutes, until golden and set to the touch.
4. Remove and let cool on pan for a minute, then transfer to a cooling rack. Makes 14 to 16 cookies.

CASHEW BUTTER OATMEAL COOKIES

INGREDIENTS:
- 2 Tbsps. honey or maple syrup
- 1 Tbsp. black strap molasses
- 2 Tbsps. organic coconut oil
- ¼ cup almond milk (*or any nut milk*)
- 1/3 cup cashew butter (*blend cashew with a tip of water until smooth and you have your own home-made cashew butter*)
- 2 cups rolled oats (*pre-baked for 2 hours at low temp*)
- 1/3 cup shredded coconut
- pinch of sea salt

DIRECTIONS:
1. In a small saucepan over medium heat, combine the honey, coconut oil, nut milk and cashew butter. Whisk together and let it come to a boil for one minute. Remove from heat and stir in salt, oats, and coconut with a wooden spoon until well combined.
2. Drop dough with a cookie scoop on parchment paper lined baking sheet or a plate.
3. Refrigerate for at least 20 minutes until set. Store in refrigerator and enjoy as dessert or warm up in the morning and have with fruits for breakfast.

COCONUT ALMOND FLAX COOKIES

INGREDIENTS:
- ½ cup chopped almonds
- ¼ cup ground flax seeds
- ¾ cup pure warm water
- ¼ cup organic raisins
- ⅛ cup dried cranberries
- ¼ cup coconut oil
- ½ cup raw honey or agave or maple syrup
- ¼ tsp sea salt
- ½ cup coconut flour
- 1 cup whole wheat or spelt flour
- 1 ½ cups grated coconut

DIRECTIONS:
1. Preheat oven to 375°F. Toast almonds (*for a crunchier bite*) on a cookie sheet for about 6–8 minutes.
2. Mix ground flax seed (*freshly ground*) with warm water and let stand for 4–5 minutes to thicken.
3. Make coconut oil, honey, salt and flax seed mixture. Stir in coconut flour, spelt flour, coconut flakes and almonds. Let batter rest for 4–5 minutes to allow it to thicken slightly.
4. Place spooned sized batter mounds about 1 inch apart on parchment paper lined over a cookie sheet.
5. Bake in preheated oven for 25 minutes or until lightly browned.
6. Place cookies on cooling rack and allow to cool completely. Makes about 2 dozen cookies.

GINGER CARROT OATMEAL RAISIN COOKIES

INGREDIENTS:
- ½ cup whole wheat pastry flour or spelt flour
- 1 cup rolled oats
- 1 cup shredded coconut
- ½ tsp sea salt
- 1 tsp ground coriander powder
- 2 Tbsps. ground flax seeds
- 2 cups shredded carrots
- ½ cup organic raisins
- ½ cup cold pressed coconut oil
- ¼ cup raw honey
- 1 Tbsp. molasses
- 1 tsp fresh grated ginger

DIRECTIONS:
1. Preheat oven to 350°F. Line two baking sheets with parchment paper.
2. In a large bowl stir in flour, salt, oats, coriander, and flax seed powder. Add carrots, coconut, and organic raisins.
3. In a small bowl whisk honey or maple syrup, coconut oil and ginger to combine. Add to the flour mixture and stir until combined. Place tablespoons full onto prepared baking sheets.
4. Bake in the oven for 35 minutes or until the cookies are golden on top and bottom.
5. Transfer to a wire rack to cool completely. *Makes 25 bite-size cookies. Enjoy as breakfast or lunch. Excellent treat for children.*

GINGER OATMEAL RAISIN COOKIES

INGREDIENTS:
- 2 very ripe bananas (*around ⅔ cup*)
- 2 Tbsps. maple syrup
- 2 Tbsps. coconut oil
- 1 ½ cups roasted rolled oats
- 2 Tbsps. flax seed grounded
- 1 tsp. coriander powder
- ½ tsp. ground cardamom
- 3–4 dates chopped
- ¼ cup organic raisins
- 1 ½ Tbsps. fresh ginger finely chopped
- 4–5 crushed walnuts

DIRECTIONS:
1. Preheat oven to 350°F.
2. In a large mixing bowl, mash ripe bananas until smooth. Add olive oil and maple syrup and stir to blend.
3. Mix in oats, flax seed, Ceylon cinnamon and cardamom, and stir gently until combined.
4. Fold in your dates, organic raisins, ginger, and walnuts. Scoop out a heaping tablespoon of the dough and form into a ball. Place on a cookie sheet lined with parchment paper.
5. The cookies will not change in size, so don't worry about putting them too close together.
6. Bake cookies at 350°F for 15–20 minutes. They will be lightly browned and puffed. Makes 24 cookies.

SWEET POTATO BANANA COCONUT COOKIES

INGREDIENTS:
- 2 cups roasted oats (*blend to medium course texture*)
- ¼ cup coconut milk
- 1 cup mashed sweet potato
- 2 ripe bananas mashed
- 1 cup fine unsweetened coconut
- 3 Tbsps. honey
- ¼ tsp sea salt
- ¼ tsp coriander seed powder
- 4 Tbsps. organic raisins

DIRECTIONS:
1. Preheat oven to 300°F.
2. Add all ingredients to a bowl and mix well.
3. Use your hands to form dough into 12 equal sized balls, then shape each ball into a cookie.
4. Bake for 15 minutes.

ALMOND BUTTER COCONUT OATMEAL COOKIES

INGREDIENTS:
- ⅔ cup cold pressed coconut oil
- 1 cup natural chunky almond butter
- ¾ cup raw honey or maple syrup
- 4 Tbsps. flax seed gel
- 1 tsp pure vanilla
- ¼ cup shredded coconut
- 3 cups roasted rolled oats
- 1 ¼ cups spelt flour
- 1 tsp arrowroot powder
- 2 Tbsps. wheat germ
- ¼ cup coconut milk or water
- ¼ tsp sea salt

DIRECTIONS:
1. Preheat oven to 375° F. Beat together oil and almond butter.
2. Add flax gel, coconut milk, honey, and vanilla and beat until mixed. Stir in coconut and wheat germ.
3. In separate bowl mix together oats, flour and arrowroot powder. Stir this into peanut butter mixture.
4. Drop onto a greased stainless steel baking sheet in 1 ½ tablespoons amounts.
5. Gently press to flatten and bake for 15 to 20 minutes or until lightly browned.
6. Cool on cooling rack. Makes approximately three and a half dozen cookies.

PUMPKIN SUNFLOWER SEED COOKIES

INGREDIENTS:
- 2 cups uncooked diced pumpkin
- 2 cups shredded coconut
- 1 cup rolled oats
- ¼ cup honey
- 2 Tbsps. molasses
- 2 tsps. ground flaxseed
- ¼ cup grounded sunflower seeds
- ¼ tsp. sea salt
- ¼ tsp. coriander powder
- ¼ cup coconut milk or water
- 4 Tbsps. spelt flour
- ¼ cup pumpkin seeds
- 1 Tbsp. sesame seeds

DIRECTIONS:
1. Place pumpkin and pumpkin seeds in a food processor and pulse until finely chopped.
2. Add all other ingredients and let sit for 15 minutes.
3. Form cookies and bake on lightly oiled cookie sheet or parchment paper, bake at 350°F for 30 minutes.
4. Flip cookies over and continue to bake for another 10 minutes until golden brown on both sides.

ALMOND and ORGANIC RAISINS BREAKFAST BARS

INGREDIENTS:
- 1 ¼ cup almond meal (*chop almonds to powder in blender*)
- ½ cup coconut fresh shredded (*for dried coconut flakes add a few tablespoons of water to recipe to achieve moisture*)
- ¼ cup coconut oil
- ¼ cup raw honey or maple syrup
- ¼ tsp sea salt
- 1 Tbsp. flax seed powder
- ½ cup pumpkin seeds
- ½ cup sunflower seeds
- ¼ cup almond slivers
- ¼ cup organic raisins
- ¼ – ½ cup water or nut milk

DIRECTIONS:
1. Preheat oven to 350°F. In a large bowl combine coconut oil, honey and water or nut milk.
2. In a small bowl combine almond meal (*finely ground*), sea salt and flax seed powder.
3. Stir in dry ingredients with wet then mix in coconut, almond slivers, organic raisins, pumpkin, and sunflower seeds. Grease an 8 x 8 stainless steel baking pan with coconut oil.
4. Using a scraper or wet hands press the dough evenly into the baking dish.
5. Bake at 350°F for 20–25 minutes or until golden brown. Wait for bars to cool before cutting and serving.

CAROB SPIRULINA COCONUT BALLS

INGREDIENTS:
- ¼ cup organic raisins or finely chopped dates
- ¼ cup raw cashew chopped
- ¼ cup raw honey or maple syrup
- 2 Tbsps. spirulina powder
- ¼ cup sunflower seeds
- ¼ cup pumpkin seeds
- 2 brown rice cakes crumbled, or 2 Tbsps. leftover cooked brown rice
- 4 Tbsps. carob powder
- ¼ cup shredded coconut
- ½ cup raw almonds lightly chopped
- ¼ tsp sea salt
- ¼ cup purified or spring water
- 3 Tbsps. coconut oil

DIRECTIONS:
1. Place all the nuts in a food processor or blender and chop until course but not too fine.
2. Add salt, crumbled rice cakes or cooked brown rice, shredded coconut, seeds, spirulina, and carob powder.
3. Add honey and water. The mixture should begin to bind together.
4. Scoop out ball sized amount with a spoon and roll in the palm of your hands, coating each ball with shredded coconut. Place in the fridge for an hour and then enjoy!

PINEAPPLE SUNFLOWER SEEDS COBBLER

INGREDIENTS:
- 3 cups fresh pineapple chopped into cubes
- ½ cup pineapple juice unsweetened
- ¼ cup pitted dates chopped
- 2 Tbsps. lemon or lime juice
- ½ tsp. ground coriander

Topping:
- 1 ½ cup roasted rolled Oats
- ½ cup Whole Wheat Pastry Flour
- ½ cup pineapple juice unsweetened
- ¼ cup raw honey or maple syrup
- ½ tsp. ground Coriander
- ¼ tsp. ground Cardamom
- 4 Tbsps. virgin coconut oil
- 3 Tbsps. grounded sunflower seeds
- 2 Tbsps. grounded flax seeds

DIRECTIONS:
1. Preheat oven to 375°F.
2. Coat an 8x8 stainless steel baking pan or a baking dish with ¼ tsp coconut oil.
3. **Filling**: In a medium saucepan combine fresh pineapple, juice, lemon juice, dates, coriander, and cardamom. Mix ingredients by stirring, then bring to a boil over medium-high heat, cooking about 10 minutes until the dates begin to break apart. Stir frequently.
4. **Topping**: Warm coconut oil in a small saucepan, then combine oats, flour, juice, honey, coriander, sunflower and flax seeds, and cardamom in a large bowl. Once oil is warm, pour over the mixture and stir.
5. Scoop filling into baking dish, then spread the topping over the filling and bake for 30–35 minutes or until the topping is golden brown (*watch to ensure it doesn't burn*).

Enjoy warm or cold. Can be kept in refrigerator for 4–5 days.

PINEAPPLE ALMOND COCONUT SQUARES

INGREDIENTS:
- ¼ cup coconut oil
- ½ cup thinly sliced pineapple
- ¼ cup raw honey or maple syrup
- 1 ¼ cups almond meal (*Grind almonds to powder in blender to have homemade almond meal*)
- ½ tsp. sea salt
- 2 Tbsps. flax seed powder
- ½ cup coconut shredded
- ½ cup pumpkin seeds
- ½ cup sunflower seeds
- ¼ cup almond slivers
- ¼ cup organic raisins
- ¼ cup water
- ½ cup of dry roasted rolled oats
- 10–15 cashew nuts chopped into small pieces
- ½ tsp coriander powder

DIRECTIONS:
1. Preheat oven to 350°F.
2. In a large bowl combine coconut oil, honey and water.
3. In a small bowl combine almond meal, sea salt and 1 tablespoon flax seed powder. Next mix in: coconut, pumpkin seeds, oats, cashew nuts, sunflower seeds, almond slivers and organic raisins.
4. Mix the wet ingredients with the dry ingredients.
5. Grease a 10 x 10 stainless steel baking pan with coconut oil. Using scraper or wet hands to press a thin layer of dough evenly into baking dish.
6. Layout slices of pineapple until bottom of dish is covered.
7. Layer rest of dough evenly on top of pineapple, smoothing and flattening out to about 1 inch in thickness.
8. Bake at 350°F for 30 minutes, or until golden brown. Wait for bars to cool before cutting and serving.

Creams, Chutney

8 Recipes

HOMEMADE COCONUT JELLY YOGURT

INGREDIENTS:
- 2 cups of coconut jelly
- 1 Tbsp. lemon juice
- 2–3 probiotic capsules (*empty contents*) or 1 tsp probiotic powder
- Pinch sea salt
- 1 Tbsp. honey or maple syrup or coconut nectar or agave to taste (*optional*)

DIRECTIONS:
1. Place coconuts in refrigerator overnight. In the morning, scoop out jelly and place in a food processor or blender.
2. Add remaining ingredients and blend until a smooth yogurt consistency is achieved.
3. Place in refrigerator and allow to chill for one hour or more. Serve with fresh banana, papaya, pineapple, soursop, or other toppings of choice. (*Enjoy with homemade granola cereal*).
4. Store in refrigerator for 4–5 days

NON-DAIRY BANANA 'Nice Cream'

INGREDIENTS:
- 4 brown frozen bananas sliced
- 1/8 cup of nut milk

DIRECTIONS:
1. Place the banana slices into a food processor and pulse until creamy. (*You will need to scrape down the sides a couple of times*).
2. Once it becomes the consistency of a soft serve ice cream you are done. This will satisfy your sweet tooth.
3. Add carob chips, organic raisins, chopped nuts or fruit on top to give some more flavor (*Optional*).

PINEAPPLE ZUCCHINI 'Nice Cream'

INGREDIENTS:
- ½ medium zucchini frozen slices (*To omit any trace of 'green' flecks peel zucchini prior to freezing – optional*)
- 1 ½ cups fresh pineapple frozen chunks
- 1 ripe avocado flesh only
- ¾ cup raw unsalted cashews (*soaked for 2 hours*) rinsed and drained
- ¼ cup coconut cream (*thick part at the top after blending coconut*)
- ½ cup grated coconut
- Pinch of sea salt

DIRECTIONS:
1. Add cashews to food processor and blend until almost smooth (*not nut butter*).
2. Add avocado, frozen zucchini and pineapple chunks. Pulse until ingredients come together roughly.
3. Add coconut cream, salt and grated coconut (*Leave grated coconut to briefly pulse through at the end if you prefer bits of coconut for more texture*). Blend until smooth.
4. Place in freezer for 30 minutes. Enjoy as a dessert after lunch with toasted coconut and pineapple toppings just before serving.

SPIRULINA 'Nice Cream'

A delicious and nutritious vegan ice cream the entire family will love. *I always keep a few frozen bananas ready to go for this recipe or to add to my fruit smoothies.*

INGREDIENTS:
- 3 ripe bananas, peeled, cut into 2-inch pieces and frozen in zip lock bag
- 2 tsps. spirulina powder
- Nuts and organic raisins for topping

DIRECTIONS:
1. Blend bananas and powder together until smooth.
2. Sprinkle on toppings and serve.

BANANA, STRAWBERRIES and COCONUT JELLY CREAM

INGREDIENTS:
- ½ cup strawberries fresh or frozen
- 2 ripe bananas
- ½ cup coconut jelly
- Pinch sea salt
- Dash coriander powder
- ½ cup water

DIRECTIONS:
1. Place all ingredients in a blender and blend until smooth.

CASHEW BANANA LEMON CREAM

INGREDIENTS:
- ½ cup raw cashews
- 2 Tbsps. honey or maple syrup
- 2 Tbsps. lemon juice
- 2 Tbsps. virgin coconut oil
- 1 large or 2 small ripe bananas
- ½ cup of pure water

DIRECTIONS:
1. Put all ingredients in blender and blend until smooth.
2. Pour into a container and place in refrigerator to set for 30 minutes.
3. Use on muffins, home-make granola, bread etc. Will last in the fridge for 5–7 days.

OTAHEITE APPLE COCONUT CREAM

INGREDIENTS:
- 1 apple
- 1 Tbsp. ground sesame seeds
- Dash of Celtic Sea salt
- 1 cup coconut milk

DIRECTIONS:
1. Blend until smooth and serve.

TROPICAL JAMAICAN MANGO CHUTNEY

INGREDIENTS:
- 2 large ripe mangos peeled, pitted and diced
- 1 medium pineapple diced
- ½ cup golden organic raisins
- 3 Tbsps. raw honey or maple syrup
- ¼ tsp grated ginger
- ½ tsp ground cumin
- ½ tsp coriander powder
- 1 cup grated coconut
- ½ cup roasted peanuts or almonds
- ½ tsp sea salt

DIRECTIONS:
1. In a medium saucepan, combine the mango, pineapple, organic raisins, ginger, water, honey, cumin, and coriander.
2. Bring to a boil. Reduce heat and simmer for 15 minutes.
3. Stir in remaining ingredients and simmer over low heat for 30 minutes more until thickened (*add water if necessary*).
4. Serve with your favorite fresh salad, roasted Irish potatoes, bean, and brown rice or just have with toasted whole wheat bread.

Cakes, Brownie

8 Recipes

VEGETARIAN RAW CARROT CAKE BITES

CARROT CAKE
- 2 ½ cups shredded carrots (*about 3–4 large carrots*)
- 1 cup raw walnuts
- 1 cup pitted dates or organic raisins
- ½ cup shredded coconut
- ¾ tsp coriander powder
- Pinch of sea salt

CASHEW CREAM FROSTING
- 1 cup raw cashews soaked overnight
- ¼ cup pure water
- 3 Tbsps. raw agave nectar or raw honey
- ½ lemon juiced
- ⅓ cup coconut oil
- pinch of salt

DIRECTIONS:
1. Line 8 x 8 baking pan or equivalent sized loaf pan with parchment paper so that the edges hang over the sides.
2. By hand or in a food processor with the grating attachment, shred carrots. Place in large bowl and set aside.
3. Blend walnuts and dates together into small chunks. Add coconut, coriander and salt and blend.
4. Add carrots and blend until well combined, scraping down the sides often. Scoop cake into prepared pan, smooth top, and chill.
5. **To make cashew cream:** drain and rinse-soaked cashews in clean water. In a food processor or blender combine cashews, water, agave nectar, salt, and lemon juice.
6. Blend **VERY WELL**, scraping down the sides often, until **VERY SMOOTH**.
7. Depending on the strength of your blender this may take up to 10 minutes. Add coconut oil and blend to combine.
8. Spoon onto chilled cake and smooth the top. Place in refrigerator for 2 hours.
9. Pull from fridge and remove cake from pan by pulling up the sides of the parchment paper.
10. With sharp knife cut cake into (*approximately*) 1 x 2 inch pieces.
11. Decorate with walnuts and sprinkle with coriander powder.

CAROB COCONUT BANANA CAKE

INGREDIENTS:

Cake:
- 4 large ripe bananas
- 1 ½ cups coconut milk
- ½ cup coconut oil
- ¼ cup grated coconut
- 2 cups whole wheat pastry or Spelt flour
- ¼ cup maple syrup, raw honey, or stevia plant sugar
- 1 cup unsweetened carob powder
- 5 Tbsps. ground flaxseed
- 1 tsp. coriander powder
- 1/4 tsp. sea salt
- 2 Tbsps. pumpkin seeds
- 2 Tbsps. sunflower seeds
- ¼ cup dry roasted rolled oats

Frosting:
- ¼ cup coconut oil
- 1 tsp. sunflower seed lecithin
- 1 cup maple syrup or honey
- 1 Tbsp. black strapped molasses
- ½ cup carob powder
- ¼ cup grated coconut
- ½ cup coconut milk
- Dash of sea salt

DIRECTIONS:

1. Preheat oven to 350°F and lightly spray two 8-inches round stainless-steel cake pans or glass bakeware or one large rectangular stainless-steel pan with nonstick coconut oil spray. Dust with carob powder, shake out excess and set aside. Mix coconut milk and oil in a large mixing bowl. Add mashed ripe bananas and beat until combined.
2. Add flour, carob powder, oats, grated coconut, grounded flaxseeds, coriander, seeds, and salt to wet ingredients while mixing with a hand-held or standing mixer. Beat until no large lumps remain. It should be chunky and pourable. Taste and adjust sweetness as needed, adding more honey if desired.

3. Divide batter evenly between your 2 smaller cake pans or 1 large rectangular pan.
4. Bake 35–45 minutes (*35 minutes for small cakes, 45 minutes for one large cake*), or until a toothpick inserted into the center comes out clean. Let cool completely before frosting.
5. While cooling, prepare frosting by beating together all ingredients until light and fluffy, adding honey or maple syrup in small amounts until you reach your desired consistency and sweetness. If it becomes too thick, add more coconut milk. If it's too thin, add more carob powder.
6. Once cake is cooled, frost generously with frosting, adding a thick layer between the top and bottom layers (*if doing a 2-layer cake*). Alternatively, omit frosting and dust with carob powder.

CASHEW VEGAN CHEESECAKE

INGREDIENTS:
- 2 cups raw cashews soaked, rinsed and drained
- 1 cup almond meal
- ¾ cup dates (*de-pitted*)
- 1 ½ lemons juiced
- ¼ cup maple syrup or organic raw agave
- ½ cup cherries or strawberries (*de-pitted*) or pineapple
- ¼ cup cold pressed apple juice or water

DIRECTIONS:
1. For crust, blend almond meal and dates until mixture sticks together. Press mixture into a 6 or 8-inch pie dish. For filling, blend cashews, lemon juice, maple syrup until silky smooth. Scoop filling over crust.
2. Freeze for at least two to three hours.
3. For topping, blend cherries and strawberries or slice pineapple thin and spread over top of pie.
4. Add a little maple syrup to adjust sweetness (*optional*).
5. Defrost cheesecake in fridge for 45–60 minutes, until the center is cold but not frozen.
6. Slice and serve with a hearty drizzle of fruit topping.
7. Once pie is completed, place back in fridge and enjoy as a cold desert after a meal.

CAROB MANGO VEGAN CHEESECAKE

INGREDIENTS:
- 2 cups raw cashews soaked, rinsed, and drained
- 1 cup almond nuts
- ¼ cup pecan nuts
- ¾ cup dates (*de-pitted*)
- 2 lemons juiced
- ¼ cup maple syrup or raw honey
- ½ cup mangoes sliced and coconut shredded (*for topping*)
- ¼ cup cold pressed apple juice or water
- ¼ cup virgin coconut oil
- ¼ cup carob powder
- 3 Tbsps. tahini
- ¼ tsp sea salt

DIRECTIONS:
1. **For crust**: Blend almond and pecan nuts to a meal like consistency. Add dates and mix in food processor until mixture sticks together. Press mixture into a 6 or 8-inch pie dish.
2. **For filling**: blend cashews, lemon juice, coconut oil, maple syrup and sea salt until silky smooth. Put some shredded coconut over crust then scoop filling over it. Place in fridge for at least two to three hours to set.
3. **For topping**: slice mangoes thinly and layer over cake. Sprinkle shredded coconut below and on top of mango slices. Add a little maple syrup to adjust sweetness (*optional*).
4. Slice and serve with a hearty drizzle of fruit topping.

CAROB COCONUT CAKE

INGREDIENTS:
- 3 Tbsps. Tahini paste
- ¼ cup prunes (*blended*)
- ¼ cup organic raisins
- ½ tsp sea salt
- 5 Tbsps. flax seed meal powder
- ½ cup grated coconut
- ¼ cup carob powder
- ¼ tsp coriander powder
- 1 tsp non-alcoholic vanilla
- 2 cups Spelt flour
- 3 Tbsps. coconut oil
- 2 Tbsps. pumpkin and sunflower seeds
- ¼ cup pecans (*break into small bits*)
- Four Brazil nuts (*chopped*)
- 1 cup water

DIRECTIONS:
1. In a bowl combine all wet ingredients, slowly mixing in dry ingredients one at a time.
2. Mix until all ingredients are fully combined.
3. Pour in baking dish (*glass or stainless steel*) which has been greased with coconut oil.
4. Bake in oven at 300°F for 45 minutes.

ALMOND MIXED FRUITS CAKE

INGREDIENTS:
- 2 cups almond paste (*or blend out 2 cups-soaked almonds*)
- 2 cups spelt four
- 1 cup mixed fruits (*mangoes, pineapple, peach, and strawberries*)
- 1 tsp coriander
- ¼ cup organic raisins
- 1 tsp sea salt
- ¼ cup flaxseed powder
- ½ cup toasted oats
- 3 Tbsps. raw honey
- 2 Tbsps. virgin coconut oil
- ½ cup coconut milk or water

DIRECTIONS:
1. In a mixing bowl, pour in dry ingredients, then add all wet ingredients, combine using a large spoon.
2. Pour into two 8 x 8 baking dishes. Bake for 1 hour at 350°F or until sticking a knife in the middle of cake comes out dry. You can also add nut and grated coconut to recipe.

SIMPLE VEGAN CARROT CAKE

INGREDIENTS:
- 3 cups raw carrots shredded
- 9 Tbsps. flaxseed gel (*to replace 3 eggs*)
- 1 ¾ cups raw honey or maple syrup
- 2 ½ cups spelt or rye flour
- ½ cup coconut oil
- 1 tsp coriander powder (*to replace cinnamon*)
- ½ tsp cardamom powder (*to replace nutmeg*)
- ¼ tsp grated ginger
- 3 tsps. arrowroot powder
- ½ tsp sea salt
- ¼ cup shredded coconut

DIRECTIONS:
1. Combine shredded raw carrot, coconut and honey in a bowl and mix well.
2. Add flaxseed gel, then oil and vanilla and mix well.
3. Combine and sift together flour, coriander, cardamom, ginger, along with arrowroot powder and salt.
4. Slowly add dry ingredient combination to wet mixture and mix until completely combined. (*If you have a food processor it makes this easier and quicker – put all wet ingredients in first, then add all dry ingredients, pulse until combined.*)
5. Pour batter into greased stainless steel baking container or glass baking dish and bake for about 40 minutes at 350°F or until you stick a knife in the center and it comes out dry.

BLACK BEAN CAROB BROWNIE

INGREDIENTS:
- 1 cup quinoa flour (*or spelt, rye or garbanzo flour – however these would require a longer baking time of 60 minutes*)
- ⅓ cup cane sugar (*low GI for diabetes, use honey if not diabetic*)
- 2 cups black beans (*16 ounces*) cooked and drained
- 3 Tbsps. flaxseeds
- ¼ cup sunflower seeds
- ¼ cup walnuts
- ½ cup carob powder
- 3 Tbsps. virgin coconut oil
- 1 tsp. vanilla extract
- ¼ cup pureed prunes
- ¾ cup coconut milk
- ½ cup grated coconut
- 2 Tbsps. arrowroot powder
- ½ tsp. sea salt
- ¼ tsp. coriander
- ¼ tsp. cardamom

For Topping:
- ¼ cup organic raisins
- 1 Tbsp. pumpkin seed grounded
- 1 Tbsp. carob powder
- ¼ cup walnuts chopped

DIRECTIONS:
1. Preheat oven to 350°F. Lightly coat a 9 x 9 baking pan with cooking spray.
2. In food processor, add black beans, carob powder and oil. Cover and process until well blended.
3. Add cane sugar, ½ of the walnuts, sunflower seeds, arrowroot powder, grounded flaxseeds, coriander, cardamom, and salt. Cover and process again until smooth. Transfer into prepared baking pan.
4. Mix remaining crushed walnut, organic raisins, crushed pumpkin seeds in a tablespoon of carob powder and pour mixture on top of your whole Brownie, using a spoon to spread out evenly.
5. Bake in preheated oven for 35 minutes or until a toothpick inserted near the center comes out clean.
6. Let cool on wire rack. Cut into bars. Ready to be served.

Patties, Burgers, Loaves

14 Recipes

CARROT and NUT PATTIES

INGREDIENTS:
- ½ cup shredded carrots
- ½ cup boiling water
- ½ cup oats and wheat bran
- 2 Tbsps. flax seeds (*freshly grounded*)
- 1 tsp garlic powder
- ½ tsp crushed sage or fennel seeds
- ¼ tsp sea salt
- 2 stalks scallion
- 2 tsps. maple syrup
- ¼ cup pecans or walnuts (*grounded in blender*)
- 1 tsp black strap molasses
- ¼ tsp fresh thyme leaves

DIRECTIONS:
1. Stir together flax seeds and boiling water and set aside to soak for 5 minutes.
2. Add oats, bran, shredded carrot, nuts, and dry spices. Stir to combine.
3. Add scallion and thyme with all other ingredients – mix well.
4. With your hands, form mixture into ½" thick patties. Heat oven to 350°F.
5. Lay patties on a stainless-steel baking sheet (*or place parchment paper over your regular baking sheet*).
6. Bake patties for 15 minutes on one side, then flip over and finish until the other side becomes golden brown.

If you don't have an oven the patties can be done on the stove top as follows:
1. Heat a quarter inch of olive or coconut oil in a cast iron pan.
2. When oil is hot, fry patties for a few minutes on each side, until golden.
3. Repeat last step with remaining batter, adding more oil each round as necessary.
4. Serve warm with whole grain bread, roasted breadfruit or a vegetable salad.

IRISH POTATO VEGETABLE PATTIES

INGREDIENTS:
- ½ cup grated Zucchini
- ½ cup grated Carrot
- 1 cup grated Irish Potato
- 4 Tbsps. Oats flour
- 2 Tbsps. Flaxseed meal
- ½ tsp. sea salt
- 4 Tbsps. Hot water
- Herbs of your choice: garlic, onion, scallion, dill, sage, coriander, parsley etc.
- 2 Tbsps. Coconut oil

DIRECTIONS:
1. Place all grated vegetables in a bowl, add coconut oil and water, then add flaxseed meal, salt and herbs and mix with a fork. Use a spoon to scoop out the amount needed to make a ball.
2. Flatten with fork and layer patties on baking sheet lined with parchment paper. Bake at 300°F for 35 minutes.

PINTO BEANS and CORN VEGGIE BURGER

This recipe makes 4 burgers.

INGREDIENTS:
- ½ cup onion diced
- ½ cup dry whole wheat breadcrumbs
- ¼ cup cilantro or parsley chopped
- 2 Tbsps. bell (*sweet*) pepper diced
- 2 Tbsps. cashew nuts
- 2 Tbsps. Lemon or lime juice
- ½ tsp ground cumin
- 1 scallion stalk
- ⅛ tsp salt
- 4 Tbsps. flax seed gel
- 2 cups pinto beans cooked
- 1 cup whole kernel corn cooked

Toppings:
- Home-made tomato sauce
- Red onion slices
- Tomato slices
- Baby spinach leaves
- Whole wheat or sprouted wheat hamburger buns

DIRECTIONS:
1. To prepare burgers, combine the first 9 ingredients in a food processor (*this saves on time if you have a good food processor*). Transfer to a large bowl and mix in flax seed gel.
2. Place pinto beans and corn in food processor, and then add to mixture in bowl.
3. Alternatively, you can add pinto beans or corn to bowl and partially mash with a fork or potato masher.
4. Divide mixture into 4 equal portions, shaping each portion into 3 ½ inch patties. Refrigerate for 10 minutes.
5. Bake for 20 minutes (*10 minutes on each side*) or prepare on top of stove by heating olive or coconut oil in a large nonstick skillet over medium-high heat.
6. Add patties to pan and cook 5-10 minutes on each side or until thoroughly heated through.

KIDNEY BEANS BURGERS

INGREDIENTS:
- 2 cups cooked kidney beans (*soaked overnight and slow cooked for two hours*)
- 1 cup tomatoes chopped
- 3 medium red onions
- ¼ cup grounded flax seed
- 6 Tbsps. rolled oatmeal
- Large handful of fresh cilantro or parsley
- 2 stalks scallion
- ¼ tsp of sea salt to taste
- ¼ tsp of sage, cumin, basil herbs

DIRECTIONS:
1. Chop onions finely, and fry for a couple of minutes to soften. Leave to cool. Drain water off cooked kidney beans.
2. In food processor place beans, tomatoes, oatmeal, soy sauce and flax seed. Whizz until chopped and combined.
3. Remove mixture from processor into a large bowl and stir together with other ingredients.
4. Form into patties by taking a heaped dessert spoonful of mixture, rolling it into a ball between your hands, then flattening it. Bake at 350°F for 15 minutes on each side, until cooked through (*the sides will be slightly brown*).
5. Served in whole grain bread rolls with your choice of garnish (*salad, nut cheese or tomato sauce*).

Uncooked burgers can be wrapped in parchment paper and stored in freezer. Pop two in the oven when you are ready for 20 minutes.

PUMPKIN OATS BURGERS

Makes 4 patties.

INGREDIENTS:
- 1 cup rolled oats roasted
- ¾ cup pumpkin puree or fresh pumpkin mashed
- 1 Tbsp. hemp seeds
- 1 Tbsp. flax seeds
- ¼ cup unsalted sunflower seeds
- 1 tsp mixed herbs (*basil, sage, parsley, etc.*)
- 2 scallion stalks diced
- ¼ tsp onion powder
- ¼ tsp garlic powder
- ½ tsp sea salt

DIRECTIONS:
1. Pulse ingredients together in food processor. *(For smoother patties, blend oats and seeds until powdery before adding remaining ingredients. I left mine with chunks of whole seeds and oats for added crunch)*.
2. Divide and form mixture into 4 patties. Place on a greased cookie sheet.
3. Bake at 300°F for 20 minutes, or until the edges become crispy. The center should still be soft.
4. Spread some hummus on a whole grain bun, add a pumpkin patty and then top with a handful of spinach, lettuce and a few onion rings or top with slices of tomato and a few rings of onion. Or pair your patty with a bed of spinach and vegan nut 'cheese' spread with a drizzle of lemon juice.

OATS PECAN BURGERS

INGREDIENTS:
- 5 cups water
- ⅓ cup extra-virgin olive oil
- 1 cup pecan chopped
- 2 tsps. garlic powder
- 1 ½ tsps. basil dried or fresh
- ½ tsp oregano dried or fresh
- 2 tsps. onion powder
- 1 tsp cumin
- ½ tsp caraway seed powder
- 1 tsp coriander powder
- 2 cups roasted rolled oats or millet grain
- 2 cups quick oats
- 2 cups cooked brown rice
- 1 tsp sea salt
- 3 Tbsps. grounded flax seed

DIRECTIONS:
1. Bring all ingredients to a boil (*except oats and rice*). Then add oats and brown rice and cook on low for 5 minutes stirring constantly.
2. Remove from heat and cover pan to allow mixture to cool to room temperature.
3. Using a canning jar lid, mold burger mixture according to desired size. Then place burgers on a cookie sheet covered with parchment paper and bake them at 350°F for 35 minutes.
4. These burgers can be kept for 4–5 days in refrigerator and much longer in the freezer.

GUNGO PEAS BURGERS

INGREDIENTS:
- 2 ½ cups quick oats
- 2 cups cooked Gungo peas (*green or dried*) mashed
- 1 ½ cups coconut milk
- ½ cup sunflower seeds ground
- ½ cup whole grain breadcrumbs
- ½ cup minced onion
- ½ tsp sage powder
- ½ tsp onion and garlic powders
- 2 cloves garlic chopped
- ½ tsp kelp powder (*purchase at any health food store*)
- ½ tsp sea salt

DIRECTIONS:
1. Mix all ingredients well, adding coconut milk a little at a time to ensure that mixture does not get too moist. Make into patties and bake at 375°F on parchment paper in a baking dish for 45–60 minutes.

LENTIL BURGERS with FRUIT SALSA

INGREDIENTS:

Fruit Salsa:
- ¼ cup pineapple finely chopped
- ¼ cup mango finely chopped
- ¼ cup tomato finely chopped
- 1 Tbsp. fresh lime juice
- ¼ cup red onions finely chopped

Burgers:
- 1½ cups pure water
- ½ cup dried lentils
- 3 Tbsps. coconut oil
- 1 cup onion chopped
- ¼ cup carrot grated
- 2 tsps. minced garlic
- 2 Tbsps. tomato paste

- 1½ tsps. ground cumin
- ¾ tsp dried oregano
- ¾ tsp sea salt divided
- ¼ cup flax seeds grounded
- ¼ cup fresh parsley finely chopped

DIRECTIONS:
1. To prepare *fruit salsa*, combine first 5 ingredients. Cover and refrigerate.
2. To prepare *burgers*, combine water and lentils in a saucepan. Bring to a boil.
3. Cover, reduce heat and simmer for 25 minutes or until are tender. Drain and place half of lentils in a large bowl. Place remaining lentils in a food processor. Process until smooth. Add processed lentils to whole lentils in bowl. Heat a large nonstick skillet over medium high heat. Coat pan with coconut oil.
4. Add onion and carrot. Sauté for 2 minutes or until tender, stirring occasionally.
5. Add garlic. Cook 1 minute, stirring constantly.
6. Add tomato paste, cumin, oregano, sage, and ¼ teaspoon salt. Cook for 1 minute, stirring constantly.
7. Add onion mixture to lentils. Add remaining salt, flax seeds, and all other ingredients. Stir well.
8. Cover and refrigerate 20 minutes or until firm.
9. Divide mixture into 8 portions, shaping each into ½ inch thick patties.
10. Heat 1½ tablespoons oil in a large nonstick skillet over medium high heat.
11. Add 4 patties. Cook for 3 minutes on each side or until brown.
12. Repeat procedure with remaining 1½ tablespoons oil and 4 patties. Serve with salsa.
13. If you want to use less oil in your cooking bake your patties by spreading them out on a baking sheet and bake on each side for 10 minutes.

PUMPKIN-SUNNY SEED LOAF

INGREDIENTS:
- 2 ½ cups water
- 2 ½ cups quick oats
- 1 cup grated coconut
- ¾ cup sunflower seeds
- ¾ cup pumpkin seeds
- 2 onions chopped
- 2 cloves garlic diced
- 2 tsp. sea salt
- 2 Tbsps. honey or maple syrup (*optional for a sweet loaf*)

DIRECTIONS:
1. Grind sunflower and pumpkin seeds in blender with 1 ½ cups water. Pour into a bowl.
2. Use remaining water to rinse blender. Add all other ingredients to bowl and mix thoroughly.
3. Allow to sit for 10 minutes in a 9 x13 oiled casserole dish.
4. Spread evenly and bake at 350°F for 45 minutes covered and another 15 minutes uncovered.

CARROT and RED LENTILS FRITTERS

INGREDIENTS:
- 1 cup grated carrots
- 1 cup oven slow baked Spelt flour or Breadfruit flour
- ½ cup cooked Red Lentil (*found at some supermarkets or health food store, if not, use regular lentils*)
- ¼ cup virgin coconut oil (*only needed if frying fritters*)
- ½ tsp sea salt
- Herbs: sage, parsley, basil, turmeric, oregano, cumin
- 1 small onion diced
- 3 stalks scallion diced
- 2 tsps. flaxseeds grounded
- ¼ cup coconut milk or water

DIRECTIONS:
1. Put Spelt flour in baking dish and place in oven for 1 hour at 200°F.
2. In a bowl, put all dry ingredients, and then add herbs, onion, salt and scallion.
3. Add coconut milk or water slowly until you get a nice fritter texture (*not too dry or wet*).
4. No need for oil if using stainless steel frying pan or griddle, however if using glass or ceramic frying pan, add coconut oil and allow to get hot on medium heat, then using a tablespoon scoop up fritter batter and place each spoonful into the hot oil.
5. Let it fry on each side for 4–5 minutes. You can enjoy these with avocado and raw vegetable salad.

LENTIL WALNUT LOAF

INGREDIENTS:
- 1 cup organic brown lentils
- 4 cups water
- 1 bay leaf
- 2 Tbsps. coconut oil
- 1 small onion
- 2 cloves garlic
- 1 small red or yellow bell pepper
- 1 medium carrot shredded
- 1 celery stalk
- 2 Tbsps. fresh parsley
- 1 tsp sea salt
- ½ tsp sage
- ½ tsp marjoram
- 2 Tbsps. grounded flax seeds
- 1 cup chopped walnuts
- 4 Tbsps. organic tomato paste
- 1 cup whole grain breadcrumbs or roasted oats crumbs

Topping:
- 2 Tbsps. organic tomato paste
- 2 Tbsps. lemon juice
- 2 Tbsps. pure maple syrup

DIRECTIONS:
1. Wash and drain lentils. Place in pan with 3 cups of fresh water and bay leaf.
2. Bring to a boil. Simmer on low for 20 minutes or until lentils are soft.
3. Most of the cooking liquid should dissipate. (*If not, drain lentils in a colander*). Place cooked lentils in large bowl.
4. Chop onion, garlic, bell pepper, celery, carrot and parsley in food processor.
5. Sauté vegetables in coconut oil until soft. Add to lentils. Stir in salt and other seasonings. Add grounded flax seeds and combine.
6. Stir in chopped walnuts, tomato paste and bread crumbs. Gently combine all ingredients, then add one cup of water. Pour into oiled loaf pan.

To make topping:
1. Stir together tomato paste, lemon juice and maple syrup until smooth. Gently spread over loaf.
2. Cover loaf with cookie sheet and bake at 350°F for 25 minutes.
3. Uncover and bake 10 to 15 more minutes until golden brown.
4. Lentil Loaf can be served with a fresh salad, over steamed brown rice or with mashed Irish potatoes.

MIXED PEAS LOAF

INGREDIENTS:
- 3 cups cooked peas (*lentils, chickpeas*) of your choice
- 3 Tbsps. grounded flaxseed
- 1 tsp onion powder
- 1 tsp garlic powder
- 1 tsp turmeric powder
- 3 Tbsps. rolled oats
- 2 cloves garlic
- 3 Tbsps. arrowroot flour
- 1/8 cup water
- Sea salt and other herbal seasonings to taste (*basil, sage, oregano, marjoram, parsley*)

DIRECTIONS:
1. Mix together the first eight (8) ingredients in a food processor for 2 minutes.
2. Dissolve arrowroot flour into water and add to the first mixture.
3. Place mixture into a 10" loaf Pyrex dish and bake for 15–20 minutes.
4. Make a tomato sauce by blending together: 2 tomatoes, 1 small onion, dash of cayenne pepper and sea salt to the taste. Pour over top of loaf and allow cooking for another 10–15 minutes.

CASHEW NUT CHEESE LOAF

INGREDIENTS:
- 3 Tbsps. spelt flour (*slow cooked for 2 hours on very low heat*)
- 1 cup cashew raw or soaked
- 4 Tbsps. grounded sunflower seeds
- 2 cloves garlic
- ½ medium onion
- 4 Tbsps. lemon juice
- Dash dried parsley, dill weed seeds, basil
- ½ tsp. sea salt
- 3 Tbsps. sesame tahini
- ½ cup red or yellow bell pepper

DIRECTIONS:
1. Blend until smooth and creamy. Pour into a small coated stainless steel baking pan or a glass baking dish and bake at 350°F for 30 minutes or until firm.
2. It will settle and get firmer as it cools. Refrigerate after and enjoy with your favorite bread or crackers.

DEHYDRATED VEGAN ACKEE QUICHE

INGREDIENTS:
- 1 cup leftover cooked vegan ackee (*or cook a fresh pot of vegan ackee with lots of onions, scallion, garlic, bell pepper, salt, cayenne pepper, fresh thyme, and tomatoes*)
- ½ cup chickpea flour
- 3 Tbsps. flaxseed powder
- 3 Tbsps. chia seeds powder
- ¼ tsp sea salt
- 1 Tbsp. coconut oil
- 2–4 Tbsps. pure water

DIRECTIONS:
1. In a medium bowl, pour in all dry ingredients. Add coconut oil and start mixing with a spoon, then add water slowly.
2. Using a large spoon add cooked ackee, folding in gently one spoon at a time.
3. Get your dehydrator sheet and cover with a sheet of parchment paper.
4. Divide recipe into two parts, scoop one part on a dehydrator sheet and spread out flat with spoon, then slice into four long strips using a sharp knife. Slice across the four strips (*giving you eight slices*).
5. Turn dehydrator to 130°F and let process for 8–10 hours.
6. If you don't have a dehydrator, bake in your oven at 300°F for 35–45 minutes or until firm and slightly crisp.

Flax Gel, Spreads, Cheese, Butter, Jams

17 Recipes

FLAX SEED GEL

NO BAKING POWDER, BAKING SODA OR EGGS. INSTEAD USE FLAXSEED GEL.

INGREDIENTS:
- ¼ cup flax seeds
- 2 cups of spring or purified water

DIRECTIONS:
1. Pour mixture into a pan and bring to a boil.
2. Stirring constantly so that it does not stick to the bottom of the pan for approximately 10 minutes.
3. Let content cool on stove top for about 60 minutes
4. Use a cheese cloth (*or cut a leg off a new stocking*) to strain out liquid. Refrigerate and store flaxseeds for later use.

Use 3–4 tablespoons of flax seed gel to replace one egg in any of your favorite recipes.

HUMMUS (CHICKPEAS) SPREAD

INGREDIENTS:
- 2 cups chickpeas (*soak overnight and cook for 30 minutes the next day*)
- ¼ cup tahini (*roasted sesame seeds sold at the Health Food Store – or you can make your own*)
- 2 Tbsps. lemon juice
- 1 Tbsp. olive or cold pressed coconut oil
- 2 scallion stalks
- 2 cloves garlic peeled
- 1 tsp grounded cumin powder
- Pinch cayenne pepper
- ½ tsp garlic powder (*optional*)
- ½ tsp onion powder (*optional*)
- 1 tsp basil leaves
- Sea salt to taste

DIRECTIONS:
1. Add all the ingredients into a food processor. Run for 2–3 minutes until mixture is smooth.
2. Serve with fresh raw vegetables (*carrot stick, cucumber sticks*) or on your whole grain bread.

CHICKPEAS (mock tuna) SPREAD

INGREDIENTS:
- 1½ cups cooked chickpeas mashed
- ½ cup fresh parsley
- 1 medium onion chopped fine
- ½ cup tofu mayonnaise
- ½ tsp sea salt
- ½ red or yellow pepper diced fine
- ½ cup celery diced fine
- 2 tsp kelp powder
- 1 scallion stalk
- Dash of herbs (dill, oregano, basil)
- 2 Tbsps. lemon juice

DIRECTIONS:
1. Mix ingredients together well.
2. Chill in refrigerator. Serve in sandwiches with cucumber, tomato or carrot and celery sticks dips.
3. Make a lovely lettuce wrap. Wash two or three lettuce leaves. Stuff with the mock tuna and enjoy.
4. This will last in refrigerator for 3–4 days.

CAROB ALMOND and HAZELNUT SPREAD

INGREDIENTS:
- ½ cup carob powder
- 1 cup roasted hazelnut nuts or almond nuts (*ground to a powder in a blender until smooth and creamy*)
- ¼ cup coconut milk
- 3 Tbsps. cold pressed coconut oil
- 2 Tbsps. almond butter
- Dash sea salt to taste

DIRECTIONS:
1. Melt carob together with coconut oil, in a sauce pot and pour into a bowl.
2. Add grounded hazelnut or almonds, coconut milk and almond butter.
3. Spoon mix into airtight, sterile glass jar and store at room temperature or in fridge.
4. It can be kept for about one month (*if you can resist eating it*). Makes 1 ¾ cups.

ALMOND NUT SPREAD

INGREDIENTS:
- 1 cup-soaked Almonds (*4 hours soaking time is ok. I love to peel them by pushing them in between my fingers and pinching the skin off, you do not need to do this step*)
- ½ cup-soaked sunflower Seeds
- 1 lemon juiced
- 2 garlic cloves crushed
- ¼ cup parsley chopped finely
- ½ bell pepper (*yellow or red*) finely chopped
- 3 stalks celery chopped in tiny pieces
- 2 green onions finely chopped
- ⅛ tsp. cayenne pepper
- ¼ - ½ tsp dulse (*seaweed available at any Health Food Store*)
- ½ tea dill dried or ⅛ cup finely chopped fresh dill
- 1 tsp kelp powder

DIRECTIONS:
1. In a food processor add ½ the nuts and seeds and blend well with dulse, lemon juice, garlic, and seasonings.
2. Add rest of nuts and seeds to mixture and pulse chop leaving a bit of chunks.
3. Add pepper, onions, parsley, and chop until mixture is fully incorporated.
4. Put in a lettuce leaf then add a tomato slice, cucumber, sprouts, etc. ENJOY. I love these sandwiches.

This is a fun raw vegan recipe to take to an office luncheon or just share with your family, wait until they have enjoyed the "Tuna" then tell them it's made with nuts.

BUTTERY ROASTED CARROT and GARLIC SPREAD

INGREDIENTS:
- ½ cup olive or coconut oil
- 2 carrots unpeeled
- 3–4 large garlic cloves
- ½ tsp. sea salt
- ¼ cup bell pepper
- Dash mixed herbs to taste)
- ¼ tsp. turmeric powder

DIRECTIONS:
1. Preheat oven to 425°F.
2. On a baking sheet, toss chopped carrots and whole garlic cloves with olive oil and a generous sprinkle of salt. Spread in an even layer and roast until tender and starting to brown for about 30 minutes, flipping once or twice.
3. Remove from oven and allow to cool.
4. Once carrots and garlic have cooled to room temperature, add them to the bowl of a food processor with the remaining ingredients. Process until smooth. Taste and adjust spices as desired.
5. Serve with whole grain crackers or bread.

BETTER THAN BUTTER SPREAD

INGREDIENTS:
- 2 cups coconut milk
- 4 Tbsps. organic cornmeal
- 1 cup pumpkin diced
- ⅛ cup sunflower seeds
- 1 tsp turmeric powder
- 2 Tbsps. cold pressed coconut oil
- ½ tsp sea salt
- 1 clove garlic
- 3 Tbsps. olive oil

DIRECTIONS:
1. Bring coconut milk to a boil on very low heat. Add cornmeal one tablespoon at a time and constantly stir.
2. Add pumpkin and stir for another two minutes.
3. Add remaining ingredients, then turn off the stove.
4. Pour the mixture into a blender and add sunflower seeds and olive oil. Add a bit of salt if desired.
5. Blend until smooth. Cool and store in the fridge. Will set and harden to the consistency of soft butter by the next morning.

CASHEW CREAM CHEESE

INGREDIENTS:
- 3 cups cashew (add ½ cup of pine nuts for a higher flavor experience if desired)
- 1 cup hot water (*for a firm cheese use less water*)
- 1 Tbsp. roasted sesame seeds (*tahini*)
- 1 tsp sea salt
- ½ tsp onion powder or 1 small onion
- ½ tsp garlic powder or 2 garlic cloves
- ½ cup red bell pepper roasted or raw (*for coloring and flavor*)
- 3 tsps. lime or lemon juice
- ⅛ tsp dill seeds
- 2 Tbsps. cold pressed coconut or olive oil

DIRECTIONS:
1. Combine ingredients in a food processor or a high-speed blender and mix or blend until smooth.
2. Leave on the counter for 12 hours covered in a glass or plastic container to age.
3. **Store in refrigerator for no more than 5 days.**

BELL PEPPER NUTTY CHEESE SAUCE

INGREDIENTS:
- 1 cup pure water
- 1 ½ tsp. sea salt
- 1 cup cashew pieces
- 1 Tbsp. onion powder
- 2 Tbsps. tahini
- 1 tsp. garlic powder
- ¾ cup red bell pepper
- 2 Tbsps. lemon juice

DIRECTIONS:
1. Blend all ingredients on high 1–2 minutes until chunky.
2. For creamy cheese, pour ingredients into saucepan and cook over medium-high. Stirring constantly until thickened. (*Not necessary to cook cheese if it will be baked*).
3. Serve on sandwiches, lasagna, baked potatoes, wraps or vegetable dip.

WHOLE GRAIN MACARONI and NUT CHEESE with BROCCOLI

INGREDIENTS:
- 2 cups whole grain macaroni shells
- ½ tsp. sea salt
- 3 cups pure water
- 2 cups broccoli washed and cut into small pieces

Nut Cheese Sauce:

Blend in a blender till creamy:
- 1 cup raw cashews
- 1 cup pure water
- 2 Tbsps. sesame seeds, unhulled or 2 Tbsps. Tahini paste

Add to mixture and blend:
- ⅓ cup chopped sweet red bell pepper or pimiento
- ¼ tsp. celery salt
- ½ tsp. turmeric powder
- 2 cloves garlic
- ½ tsp. garlic powder
- 1 small onion, chopped
- ¾ tsp. sea salt
- 2 Tbsps. lemon juice

Add to cooked macaroni shells and mix well. Add broccoli pieces on top, then bake in oven for 20–25 minutes at 300°F.

HOMESTYLE SUBSTITUTE BUTTER

INGREDIENTS:
- ¾ cup cold pressed coconut oil
- ½ cup extra virgin olive oil
- 2 Tbsps. lecithin granules
- ½ cup water
- ½ tsp sea salt

DIRECTIONS:
1. Blend oils and granules together. Add water and salt and blend again.
2. Place in refrigerator in a container with a lid until set.

PUMPKIN SEED BUTTER

INGREDIENTS:
- 1 cup raw pumpkin seeds (*Examine them and remove any what looks really dry or discolored. Smell them to ensure they are not rancid. Rancid seeds have a strong smell that is not appealing*).
- 1 Tbsp. extra virgin olive or coconut oil
- 2 tsps. raw honey or maple syrup
- Pinch sea salt

DIRECTIONS:
1. Use food processor or blender to grind pumpkin seeds into a fine powder.
2. Drizzle olive or coconut oil in slowly as you process the Pumpkin Seed powder.
3. Add more oil to make it creamier if you desire.
4. Add honey and sea salt. Mix until thoroughly blended.

MILLET PUMPKIN BUTTER

INGREDIENTS:
- 1 cup cooked millet grain
- 1 cup coconut milk
- 3 Tbsps. coconut oil
- ½ tsp. sea salt
- 2 Tbsps. Honey
- 1 tsp. onion powder
- ¼ cup diced pumpkin
- 3 Tbsps. raw cashew

DIRECTIONS:
1. Add all ingredients to blender and blend until smooth and creamy.
2. Pour into glass container with cover and refrigerate overnight.
3. Enjoy with homemade bread or biscuits or add to peas or bean stews for a nice creamy sauce or serve with raw vegetable salads.

ROASTED GARLIC BUTTER

INGREDIENTS:
- 4 garlic bulbs
- 3–4 Tbsps. extra-virgin olive oil
- ¼ tsp sea salt
- Dash of freshly chopped or dried parsley flakes

DIRECTIONS:
1. Preheat oven to 350°F.
2. Cut about a half inch off top of garlic bulb.
3. Place bulb in a small baking dish. Drizzle top with olive oil.
4. Cover dish with parchment paper and bake for 10–15 minutes.
5. When garlic is done, let it cool enough to handle. (*Should be able to just squeeze cloves out of husk*).
6. Put softened baked garlic cloves in a mixing bowl, drizzle with olive, flax seed, hemp, sesame oil.
7. Mix together with a dash of sea salt and your favorite herbs (*dill, basil, parsley etc.*) until thoroughly integrated.
8. To store, scrape mixture onto a glass or plastic container and store in your refrigerator.

The roasted garlic has a sweet nutty taste. Have it with your whole grain bread, crackers or toss it in salad dressing.

ORGANIC RAISINS and SUNFLOWER SEED BUTTER

INGREDIENTS:
- ½ cup organic raisins
- ½ cup raw sunflower seeds
- 2 Tbsps. coconut oil
- Pinch of sea salt
- ½ cup pure water

DIRECTIONS:
1. Add sunflower seeds, organic raisins, oil, water and salt to a blender.
2. Blend until smooth and creamy. Keep refrigerated.

PINEAPPLE FLAXSEED JAM

INGREDIENTS:
- 1 ½ cups pineapple, chopped in small pieces (*reserve half cup finely diced*)
- ¼ cup maple syrup or raw honey (*optional*)
- 1 Tbsp. Flaxseeds
- ½ cup orange juice or water (*as needed*)
- ¼ tsp coriander powder
- 1 tsp lemon juice

DIRECTIONS:
1. Place chopped pineapple, flax seeds, and maple syrup (*if using*) into a blender.
2. Blend on medium to high speed until preferred jam consistency is obtained. Add water or orange juice 1 Tbsp. at a time as needed to get things moving.
3. Pour contents of blender into a small saucepan and heat over medium heat until jam begins to bubble.
4. Reduce heat to low and simmer for 7 minutes, or until jam starts to thicken.
5. Add finely diced pineapple (*for a chunky jam, if not, then blend all pineapple pieces at the beginning to achieve a smooth jam*), coriander powder and lemon juice.
6. Remove from heat and pour immediately into a mason jar. Allow to cool completely and then store in the fridge for up to one week.

FIGS and ORGANIC RAISINS JAM

INGREDIENTS:
- ½ cup freshly squeezed orange juice
- ¼ cup organic raisins washed
- 6 large, dried figs chopped
- 1 Tbsp. black strapped molasses
- ¼ tsp. coriander powder
- ¼ tsp. ginger powder
- 3 Tbsps. flaxseed gel or 1 Tbsp. ground flaxseed

DIRECTIONS:
1. On medium heat, place a stainless steel or glass pot, add to pot ¼ cup orange juice, along with all other ingredients, except flaxseed or flaxseed gel. Bring to boil, then turn off stove.
2. Let sit for 5 minutes, then pour in remaining orange juice and flaxseed gel.
3. Combine with a spoon, then pour into food processor or blender, and blend until chucky or smooth, *(if too thick add a little more orange juice)* depending on the type of jam you desire.
4. Enjoy on favorite homemade bread or crackers or use as topping on cereal or porridge.

Salads, Dressings, Salsa, Mayonnaise, Ketchup

36 Recipes

PURSLANE SALAD with GRILLED CORN, RED ONION, and a CREAMY AVOCADO DRESSING

INGREDIENTS for dressing:
- 1 ripe medium avocado
- 1 cup plain coconut jelly yogurt
- ½ red onion chopped
- 3 Tbsps. fresh squeezed lime juice
- 2 Tbsps. olive oil
- 1 clove garlic smashed and minced
- 1 Tbsps. Italian parsley or cilantro
- ½ tsp sea salt

DIRECTIONS:
1. Combine all ingredients in a blender, and blend until smooth.
2. Check salt and acid levels and adjust as needed. Refrigerate and dressing will be kept for several days.

INGREDIENTS to assemble salad:
- 1 bunch purslane
- 2 ears corn grilled
- ½ red onion sliced paper thin
- Pinch sea salt

DIRECTIONS:
1. Wash purslane and trim of any large stems. Tear stems into bite–sized lengths.
2. Husk grilled corn and cut kernels off cob.
3. Toss purslane, corn, and red onion together with a pinch of sea salt in a large salad bowl.
4. Drizzle with dressing and turn to coat.

CRUNCHY TOMATO SALSA

INGREDIENTS:
- 4–6 small tomatoes diced
- 2 Tbsps. cilantro chopped
- 2 scallion stalks cleaned and trimmed
- 1 small onion chopped
- ½ lemon juiced
- 2 Tbsps. parsley
- ½ red pepper seeded and stem removed
- Sea salt to taste

DIRECTIONS:
1. Add all the ingredients into a food processor and **PULSE** for 1 minute until mixture is chunky.

CARROT POTATO DILL SALAD

INGREDIENTS:
- 3 large potatoes peeled and diced
- 2 large carrots peeled and diced
- 1 small bunch of fresh dill stems removed and chopped
- 2 Tbsps. cold pressed coconut oil
- 1 tsp. cumin seeds powder
- ½ inch ginger peeled and finely shredded
- 1 ½ tsps. coriander powder
- ½ tsp turmeric powder
- 1 ½ tsps. sea salt to taste
- ½ Tbsp. lemon juice

DIRECTIONS:
1. Heat oil in wok or pan and add cumin seeds powder. When seeds sizzle, add ginger and stir fry for 10–15 seconds.
2. Add all spices then stir for a moment. Add potatoes and carrots. Stir fry for a minute until vegetables are well coated with spices. Lower heat to low-medium.
3. Add ½ cup of hot water and dill. Cover and cook until veggies are very tender, stirring from time to time.
4. Add lemon juice. Serve with your favorite bean or peas stew, with a fresh vegetable salad.

HEARTY BEAN SALAD

INGREDIENTS:
- 1 cup kidney beans cooked and drained
- 1 cup pinto beans cooked and drained
- 1 cup black–eyed peas cooked and drained
- 1 red bell pepper chopped
- 1 cup corn cooked
- ½ bunch cilantro chopped
- 2 Tbsps. virgin olive oil
- 1 lime or lemon juiced (*about 1 ½ Tbsp.*)
- 1 garlic clove minced (*optional*)

DIRECTIONS:
1. Soak the beans and peas overnight. Cook for 1 hour, drain and cool.
2. Combine all ingredients into a bowl. Serve immediately or let chill in refrigerator.

CALLALOO and BROAD BEAN SALAD

INGREDIENTS:
- 2 cups broad beans cooked
- ½ tsp fresh thyme minced
- 1 tsp scallion chopped
- 1 bunch callaloo rinsed and cut into 1-inch strips
- 2 Tbsps. extra virgin olive oil
- Sea salt to taste

DIRECTIONS:
1. Warm up the beans and season with your favorite herbs (*basil, oregano, sage and cumin*).
2. Rinse, stem and cut callaloo into strips. Steam for 2 to 3 minutes.
3. Toss the beans with olive oil, the herbs and salt.
4. Place on a platter and drizzle with more olive oil to your taste. Serve. Enjoy.

Note: **the salad can be done in advance keeping the seasoned beans and callaloo (*you can also use kale*) separate in the fridge. Remove from fridge and let them come to room temperature then toss together and season with oil and salt to taste.**

FAVA BEAN SALAD

INGREDIENTS:
- 1 cup fava beans cooked
- 1 scallion stalk thinly sliced (*white and green parts*)
- ½ red bell pepper chopped
- Handful fresh flat-leaf parsley roughly chopped
- ½ lemon juiced
- 1 tsp maple syrup or raw honey
- 2 Tbsps. extra virgin olive oil
- Sea salt to taste

DIRECTIONS:
1. Combine beans, scallion, bell pepper and parsley in a mixing bowl.
2. In a small jar with a tight-fitting lid, combine remaining ingredients and shake well.
3. Pour the dressing over the bean mixture and stir gently to combine all ingredients.
4. Serve at room temperature or cold.

CURRIED CHICKPEA, SPINACH and ROASTED RED BELL PEPPER SALAD

INGREDIENTS:
- 2 cups chickpeas cooked
- 1 cup red peppers roasted
- 1 cup large leaf spinach
- 6 Tbsps. extra virgin olive oil
- ½ red onion diced
- 4 garlic cloves crushed
- 1 tsp. turmeric powder
- 1 tsp. cumin powder
- 1 Tbsps. black strapped molasses
- 1 lemon juiced (2 Tbsps.)
- Handful fresh mint leaves roughly chopped (½ cup)
- Handful parsley leaves finely chopped (½ cup)
- Sea salt to taste

DIRECTIONS:
1. Heat the 2 tablespoons of oil in an extra-large heavy bottomed skillet over medium low heat. Add onion and garlic.
2. Gently sweat out the onions and garlic for a minute or two. (*As soon as the garlic is fragrant and the onion is just turning translucent, add dry spices*).
3. Give everything a good stir and let cook for a minute or two so that the spices can blend in and some of the raw powdery taste removed.
4. Coarsely chop the spinach while the onions cook. When the spices have completely coated the onions and it's starting to look just a bit dry, add 2 tablespoons of cold water to the pan.
5. Quickly plunk the spinach down on top and sprinkle it with salt. Place a lid over the pan immediately and let it steam, undisturbed, for 3–5 minutes.
6. As the spinach wilts, roughly chop roasted red peppers. When the spinach has been wilting away for a few minutes add the roasted red peppers and chickpeas. Remove the pan from the heat and let the mixture cool.
7. Whisk together the remaining oil with the molasses and lemon juice until everything is combined.
8. When the chickpea mixture has cooled down to room temperature, pour the dressing overtop and toss with the freshly chopped herbs. Add salt to taste.

LIVE PLANTAIN SALAD

INGREDIENTS:
- 1 small ripe plantain cut into chunks
- 1 stalk green onion (scallion) diced
- ¼ small purple onion diced
- ¼ tsp. turmeric powder
- 1 Tbsp. extra-virgin olive oil
- 1 Tbsp. lemon or lime juice
- 1 large tomato diced
- ¼ small cucumber diced
- ¼ cup jackfruit diced
- Dash of sea salt, dried chives, cilantro or parsley

DIRECTIONS:
1. Dressing: mix lemon juice, sea salt, chives, cilantro, olive oil, turmeric together (*may add 1 teaspoon of raw honey*). In a small bowl, combine all remaining ingredients, and then pour dressing on top.
2. Let it marinate for 30 minutes then serve as a cold salad on its own, or before a meal with cooked bean or peas stew and grains.

CAULIFLOWER and BROCCOLI WARM SALAD

INGREDIENTS:
- 1 small head cauliflower chopped
- ½ small head broccoli chopped
- 1 small red or yellow bell pepper cut in strips
- 1 small onion diced
- ½ tsp sea salt
- 1 Tbsp. virgin coconut oil
- ¼ tsp parsley
- 2 cloves garlic chopped very fine
- 2 Tbsps. water
- 2 stalks scallion diced
- 1 large carrot shredded

DIRECTIONS:
1. At medium heat, place your stainless steel or glass pot with 2 tablespoons water.
2. Add onions, garlic, scallion and red or yellow bell pepper. Sauté for 1 minute.
3. Add cauliflower and let steam for 2 minutes, then add broccoli, carrot, salt, and parsley.
4. Let steam for additional 2 minutes, with lid on pot. Turn off stove and add coconut oil last, while stirring to combine all ingredients together. Serve while still hot.

BLACK BEAN AVOCADO PAPAYA MANGO COLD SALAD

INGREDIENTS:
- ½ cup diced ripe mango
- ¼ cup organic raisins
- 1 cup cooked black beans
- 3 Tbsps. chopped red onion
- ½ cup diced ripe papaya
- 2 Tbsps. chopped fresh cilantro
- 3 Tbsps. chopped parsley
- 2 Tbsps. fresh lemon or lime juice
- 1 Tbsp. virgin olive oil
- 1 tsp finely chopped green onion (scallion)
- ½ tsp ground coriander
- ¼ tsp sea salt
- ¼ cup diced bell (sweet) pepper (red or yellow)
- 1 clove garlic finely chopped
- 1 avocado pitted, peeled and chopped

DIRECTIONS:
1. Soak black beans overnight, next morning, pour off water and wash.
2. Catch fresh water and cook beans for two hours until soft and tender. Rinse with cold water; drain.
3. In large bowl, stir together all ingredients except avocado. Refrigerate until ready to serve, at least 1 hour.
4. Stir in avocado just before serving, so that it doesn't get mashed out.
5. Finish this lovely salad with a topping of some pumpkin or sunflower seeds.

This very health, delicious and colorful salad can be consumed alone, or with whole wheat pita bread, breadfruit, or whole grain crackers.

BLACK BEAN COUSCOUS SALAD

INGREDIENTS:
- 2 cups couscous
- 2 cup cooked black beans drained
- ½ cup red onion diced
- ½ cup red bell pepper diced
- 1 Tbsp. fresh parsley chopped (*for garnishing*)
- ⅓ cup homemade lemon dressing

DIRECTIONS:
1. In a medium heatproof bowl, pour 1 cup boiling water over the couscous. Cover and let sit for 10 minutes.
2. Uncover, fluff with a fork, and set aside to let cool for 5 minutes more.
3. In same bowl used to prepare couscous, add black beans, onions, bell pepper, and parsley. Stir well along with the homemade lemon dressing. Taste and adjust seasoning if you think it is necessary.

BROCCOLI and ORGANIC RAISINS SALAD

INGREDIENTS
Salad:
- 2 cups broccoli raw or lightly steamed
- ¼ cup organic raisins
- 5 Tbsps. sunflower seeds
- Pinch of sea salt
- 2 garlic cloves crushed
- 2 Tbsps. walnuts crushed

Dressing:
- Juice of 1 large lemon/ or two limes
- 2 Tbsps. honey or maple syrup
- 2 Tbsps. fresh parsley finely chopped
- 1 Tbsp. tahini

DIRECTIONS:
1. In a bowl place steamed or raw broccoli pieces, walnuts, organic raisins, sunflower seeds, salt and crushed garlic. Combine all ingredients for the dressing and pour over salad.
2. Let sit for 15 minutes to develop the flavors and get dressing to marinate into broccoli.

GUACAMOLE (AVOCADO SALAD)

Avocado is a great source of healthy unsaturated fats.

INGREDIENTS:
- 2 medium avocados
- 1½ Tbsps. lime juice freshly squeezed
- 1 garlic clove minced
- 2 Tbsps. white onion finely chopped and rinsed
- ½ scotch bonnet pepper finely chopped (*optional*)
- 1 small tomato ¼ inch diced
- Sea salt to taste

DIRECTIONS:
1. Peel and crush avocadoes in a medium sized bowl. Add all the other ingredients and stir with a spoon.
2. This salad can be eaten as is or served chilled.

SPROUTED MUNG BEAN SALAD

Sprouting: Wash 1 cup of whole green Mung beans. Place in a medium size bowl and cover with filtered water. Make sure there is at least an inch of water on top of the beans, because these beans will grow.

Rinse these beans once more in a 24-hour period, and re-cover with water. On Day 2, rinse beans again and transfer to a colander. Place a wet paper towel over the sprouts and place in a warm place (*we are mimicking an earthy underground environment*). Check in after 8-12 hours to make sure paper towel is still moist. It will take 2-3 days for beans to sprout. If you are not going to use sprouts right away, place in a jar in the fridge. If you leave them out for too many days, they will spoil.

TO MAKE SALAD:

INGREDIENTS:
- 1 cup Mung beans with green skins
- 2 large, ripened tomatoes cut in cubes
- ¼ cup diced pineapple
- 3 lettuce leaves washed and chopped
- 1 small cucumber sliced
- ¼ small red or yellow bell pepper chopped
- Hand full organic raisins

Dressing:
- 2 Tbsps. olive oil
- Juice of half lemon
- Sea salt to taste
- 1 clove garlic crushed
- Cilantro for garnish

DIRECTIONS:
1. In a bowl mix in all veggies and put as many sprouts in salad as you wish. (*I like more sprouts so sprouts make up a third of my salad as the sprouts are high in protein and combined with the vegetables gives me a perfectly balanced meal for lunch or dinner*).

FARRO GRAIN and CHICKPEAS SALAD

Farro grain also called emmer is a type of ancient wheat grain that has been eaten for thousands of years around the world. This **high-fiber food, with a lovely chewy texture** is staging a comeback as a gourmet specialty. An excellent source of protein, fiber, and nutrients like magnesium and **iron,** it's a big step up from using white rice or other refined grains in your favorite dishes. As wheat, it contains the gluten protein, which is found in the grains: wheat, barley, and rye, and is most definitely not gluten-free. Although it's become more widely available recently, offering lots of fiber, B vitamins, zinc, iron and even a good dose of protein.

INGREDIENTS:
- 1 cup whole Farro grain
- ½ cup cooked chickpeas
- ½ cup diced cucumber
- ½ cup diced tomatoes
- ¼ cup diced red and yellow bell pepper
- Handful combined fresh herbs (*basil, garlic parsley, onions, celery*)
- Extra virgin olive oil
- 1 Tbsp. honey or maple syrup
- Fresh lemon juice
- Sea Salt and dash of cayenne pepper

DIRECTIONS:
1. Whole Farro (*as opposed to cracked*) can take between 30–35 minutes to cook. Cook as you would pasta – in plenty of salted boiling water.
2. Taste and when slightly soft, drain thoroughly and set aside to cool.
3. Prepare cucumber, tomato and bell pepper, and herbs for salad.
4. When Farro has cooled completely, combine with beans and vegetables.
5. Dress with extra virgin olive oil, lemon juice, honey, salt and pepper and place in a serving bowl. Sprinkle herbs on top and serve.

BLACK EYED PEA and PUMPKIN SALAD

INGREDIENTS:
- 1 cup dried black-eyed peas (soaked overnight)
- 4 cups water
- ½ medium onion
- 2 scallion stalks
- 1 bay leaf
- ½ tsp sea salt

Pumpkin:
- 1 ½ cups ½ inch cubes sugar pumpkin or butternut squash seeded & peeled (about 6 ounces)
- 3 Tbsps. water
- 1 Tbsp. olive oil
- 1 small garlic clove minced

Salad and dressing:
- 3 Tbsps. extra-virgin olive oil
- 1 ½ Tbsps. fresh lime juice
- 1 cup red onion thinly sliced
- ¼ cup green bell pepper chopped
- ¼ cup cucumber chopped, seeded and peeled
- 1 plum tomato seeded and chopped
- 2 Tbsps. fresh basil chopped

DIRECTIONS:
1. Place peas in large saucepan. Add enough water to cover by 3 inches.
2. Let peas soak over night. Drain and return to same pan.
3. Add 4 cups water, onion, bay leaf and salt. Bring to boil.
4. Reduce heat to medium, cover peas partially and let simmer until tender for about 30 minutes. Discard bay leaf. Drain. Transfer peas to rimmed baking sheet to cool. (*This can be prepared 1 day ahead. Cover and refrigerate*).
5. Preheat oven to 400°F. Arrange pumpkin in single layer in 8x8x2-inch glass baking dish.
6. Drizzle with 3 tablespoons water and oil. Sprinkle with salt.
7. Bake until tender when pierced, turning occasionally for about 15 minutes. Add garlic. Stir to coat. Cool.

Salad Dressing and completion of Salad:
1. Whisk oil and lime juice in bowl. Season dressing with salt.
2. Combine all remaining ingredients and peas in large bowl.
3. Add dressing and toss. Add pumpkin and toss.
4. Let stand at room temperature for a few minutes.

GARBANZO BEAN and RAW KALE SALAD

INGREDIENTS:
- 1 Tbsp. lemon juice freshly squeezed
- 1 Tbsp. extra-virgin olive oil
- ½ tsp sea salt to taste
- ½ tsp ground turmeric
- Dash cayenne pepper to taste
- 2 cups kale thinly sliced (*lightly steamed and cooled*)
- 1 ½ cups cooked garbanzo beans
- 1 – 2 Tbsps. red onion finely diced
- ½ cup red bell pepper diced

DIRECTIONS:
1. Place lemon juice, olive oil, salt, turmeric and cayenne pepper in a medium sized bowl and mix well.
2. Add sliced kale to salad dressing and massage dressing into kale with your hands. (*Warning: your hands may turn a little yellow. Just wash off with soap or use plastic gloves*).
3. Add garbanzo beans, red onion and red bell pepper and mix well. Serve or refrigerate until serving.
4. This makes a great "make ahead" salad so that the dressing can marinate into the beans and kale.

MILLET WITH ONIONS and PARSLEY

INGREDIENTS:
- 1 cup millet
- 2 Tbsps. homemade vegetable broth
- 1 cup chopped onion
- ½ cup chopped fresh parsley
- ¼ tsp sea salt
- ½ tsp garlic powder
- 2 stalks scallion chopped

DIRECTIONS:
1. Place millet and 6 cups water in a large saucepan. Bring to a boil, reduce heat to medium low and simmer until tender, 15 to 20 minutes. Drain well and set aside.
2. Heat broth in a large skillet over medium heat. Add onion and scallion, cook until softened for approximately 2 minutes. Add parsley, garlic powder and salt and cook 2 more minutes.
3. Stir in cooked millet and toss gently to combine. Serve with your favorite bean, peas stew or loaf.

BULGUR TABBOULEH with CILANTRO and LIME SALAD

INGREDIENTS:
- 3 Tbsps. plus 2 tsps. olive oil divided
- 1 cup bulgur rinsed and drained
- 2 large tomatoes diced (1½ cups)
- 2 medium cucumbers peeled, seeded and diced (1½ cups)
- 2 bunches green onions white and green parts chopped (1 cup)
- ¼ cup cilantro chopped
- ½ cup lime or lemon juice
- 1 Tbsp. maple syrup or honey
- Dash sea salt to taste
- 2 cups pure water

DIRECTIONS:
1. Heat 2 tsps. oil in large saucepan over medium heat.
2. Add bulgur, and toast 3 to 4 minutes, or until dry and beginning to smell fragrant.
3. Add 2 cups water, cover, and bring to a boil. Reduce heat to medium-low and cook 15 minutes.
4. Drain off water and let cool.
5. Transfer bulgur to large bowl, and stir in honey, tomatoes, cucumbers, green onions, cilantro, lime, or lemon juice, and remaining ¼ cup oil.
6. Season with sea salt, if desired. Add diced parsley and cilantro on top just before eating. For a sweet bite add organic raisins.

VEGETABLE SALAD with TAHINI HONEY SAUCE

INGREDIENTS:
- 2 cups cabbage thinly shredded (*lightly steamed and cooled*)
- ⅓ cup carrot (*julienne - cut in thin strips*)
- ⅓ cup red bell pepper julienne
- 3 Tbsps. scallions minced (*1 medium scallion*)
- 3 Tbsps. cilantro minced
- ¼ purple onion thinly sliced
- 3 Tbsps. light sesame oil
- 1 Tbsp. Tahini
- 1 Tbsp. fresh lime juice
- 1 Tbsp. honey or maple syrup
- ¼ tsp cayenne pepper (optional)

DIRECTIONS:
1. Mix together cabbage, carrot, red pepper, scallion, onions, and cilantro.
2. Whisk together sesame oil, tahini, honey, lime juice and pepper in a small bowl.
3. Pour the dressing over the vegetables and mix thoroughly. Let sit for an hour to bring the flavors together.

HERBY CARROT and GINGER DRESSING

INGREDIENTS:
- 1/3 cup fresh dill
- 1 handful fresh basil
- 1 small ginger knob
- 2 carrots
- 1 small or ½ large avocado
- ½ lemon juiced
- 6 honey or maple syrup drops
- Sea salt to taste
- 3 Tbsps. virgin olive oil
- Few Tbsps. pure water for blending (*if necessary*)

DIRECTIONS:
1. Steam carrots for 5 minutes and cut into pieces. Peel and cut ginger into strips.
2. Cube avocado and cut up dill and basil. Add all ingredients into a blender or food processor and blend or process until well combined. (*If you have a high-powered blender, you shouldn't need the water*).
3. *A clove of garlic and a tablespoon of coconut oil for a variation on the flavor would be a lovely addition.*
4. **This recipe can be served as a dip or add a little more water to thin it out and enjoy as a dressing for salad or over a delicious bowl of cooked grains like millet or quinoa.**
5. Chop some fresh veggies into the bowl for crunch factor. Will last approximately 5 days in refrigerator.

TAHINI HONEY DRESSING

INGREDIENTS:
- ¼ cup olive oil (*to reduce calories use water instead*)
- ½ cup raw tahini (*do at home by roasting sesame seeds on your stove for 5 minutes*)
- 3 tsps. fresh lemon or lime juice
- 1 Tbsp. raw honey
- ¼ tsp sea salt
- Dash herbs (basil, parsley, oregano etc.)

DIRECTIONS:
1. Blend all ingredients in a blender until smooth, adding more water as needed (*use a mixture of water and oil if you're aiming for an extra creamy, rich dressing*).
2. Will last approximately 5 days in refrigerator.

CHICKPEA VEGETABLE SALAD with CURRIED CASHEW DRESSING

INGREDIENTS:
For the dressing:
- ⅓ cup fresh cilantro chopped
- 2 Tbsps. olive oil
- 1 Tbsp. lemon juice
- 1 ½ tsps. turmeric powder
- ¾ tsp sea salt
- ½ tsp minced garlic
- ½ cup raw cashew nuts soaked

For the salad:
- 2 cups carrot finely shredded
- ½ cup golden organic raisins
- ¼ cup red onion finely chopped
- 2 cups cooked chickpeas
- 12 cups romaine lettuce chopped

DIRECTIONS:
1. **To prepare the dressing**: In a blender place cilantro, olive oil, lemon juice, turmeric powder, sea salt, garlic and cashew nuts and blend until smooth and creamy. Set aside.
2. In a large bowl, combine carrots, organic raisins, red onion and chickpeas. Pour ½ cup dressing over the carrot mixture, tossing to coat.
3. Arrange 2 cups chopped lettuce on each of 6 plates. Drizzle each serving with 1 tablespoon dressing.
Top each serving with 1 ⅓ cups chickpea mixture.

ORANGE ORGANIC RAISINS SALAD DRESSING

INGREDIENTS:
- 2 oranges juiced (*about ½ cup*)
- 1 Tbsp. raw honey or maple syrup
- ¼ cup organic raisins
- 2 Tbsps. lemons juice
- 3 Tbsps. olive oil
- ¼ cup yellow sweet pepper
- ¼ tsp. sea salt
- Herbs: basil, parsley (*use the ones you like*)

DIRECTIONS:
1. In a blender or food processor, combine all ingredients and blend until smooth.
2. Pour into a jar container and store in refrigerator. Will last for approximately 5 days.

ORGANIC TOFU MAYONNAISE DRESSING

Silken tofu has a creamy, custard-like texture that makes it a perfect substitute for standard mayonnaise. Use organic tofu mayonnaise instead of commercial dairy mayonnaise with whole grain sandwiches and vegetable salads, or even as a dip for enjoying sliced cucumber, carrot, beet, sweet pepper or tomato. Organic tofu is an excellent source of protein, B-vitamins and is naturally low in sodium. **This recipe yields about 2 cups of tofu mayonnaise.**

INGREDIENTS:
- 1 pack Superior Organic Silken Tube Tofu (240g)
- 3 Tbsps. lemon juice
- 2 garlic cloves
- 1 small onion
- ⅛ tsp. turmeric powder
- 1 tsp. honey or maple syrup
- ⅛ tsp. cayenne (optional)
- 4 Tbsps. virgin olive oil
- ¼ – ½ tsp. sea salt
- ¼ tsp. herbs: dill, basil, parsley, oregano

DIRECTIONS:
1. Blend ingredients in a food processor or blender until smooth and creamy. Add salt and lemon juice to taste.
2. Store unused portions in a covered container or jar and refrigerate. Will last approximately 6–7 days.
3. **Can be used to make other dressings or dips**.

BASIL CASHEW PESTO DRESSING

INGREDIENTS:
- ½ cup fresh basil leaf
- 2 garlic cloves roughly chopped
- ½ cup soaked cashews
- ½ cup olive oil
- ¼ cup diced yellow bell pepper
- ¼ cup lemon juice
- ½ tsp. sea salt
- Dash garlic powder
- ¼ cup diced purple onion
- Dash cayenne pepper

DIRECTIONS:
1. In a food processor, finely chop basil, bell pepper, lemon juice, onion, garlic and cashews.
2. Slowly drizzle in olive oil. (*Use amount that will make to desired consistency*).
3. Season to taste with salt and pepper.

KALE and BEET SALAD with TAHINI ORANGE DRESSING

INGREDIENTS:
Salad:
- 1 bunch kale, *stalks removed and discarded, leaves ripped or sliced into small pieces* *(lightly steamed and cooled)*
- 1 carrot julienned finely
- 1 cup bean sprouts
- 1 small beet julienned finely
- 4 radishes sliced thinly
- 6 stalks asparagus blanched briefly
- 1 cup green cabbage thinly sliced *(lightly steamed and cooled)*
- Small handful toasted sunflower seeds
- ¼ tsp. sea salt

Tahini Orange Dressing:
- ½ lemon juiced
- 1 large or 2 medium oranges juiced
- 2 Tbsps. tahini
- 2 Tbsps. raw cashews
- 2 cloves garlic crushed
- Sea salt and freshly ground pepper to taste
- ⅓ cup avocado or olive oil

DIRECTIONS:
Salad
1. In a medium bowl, combine kale with 1 tablespoon of dressing and sea salt. Using your hands, massage kale for 1 minute or so until leaves begin to wilt.
2. Add all other vegetables and toss until just combined. Add additional dressing to your liking and sprinkle with toasted sunflower seeds.

Dressing
1. Juice oranges and lemon. In a blender, or the Bullet, blend together citrus juices, tahini, cashews, and garlic. With motor running, add oil in a slow and steady stream. Blend until smooth.

2. Taste and adjust seasoning by adding more salt if needed and a dash of cayenne pepper. If dressing is too thick, thin it out by adding a tablespoon of water, or more orange juice.
3. The dressing can be kept in the fridge for up to 1 week.

GINGER SUNFLOWER SEEDS SALAD DRESSING

Have this salad for lunch made of cabbage, spinach, lettuce, alfalfa sprouts, red onions, fresh dill and chives with this dressing.

INGREDIENTS:
- 2 inches' ginger root washed and crushed
- 1 cup water (8 oz.)
- 3 Tbsps. sunflower seeds
- 2 Tbsps. raw honey
- 2 – 3 Tbsps. lemon juice
- 1 Tbsp. olive oil
- Dash of sea salt
- ¼ tsp dried parsley and basil
- 1 tsp raw cashew nuts

DIRECTIONS:
1. Place ginger and water in a small sauce pot. Let boil for 5 minutes at low heat.
2. Turn off and allow to steep for another 5 minutes.
3. Strain off water and remove ginger, then place liquid in a blender.
4. Add all other ingredients to blender. Blend until smooth and place in fridge to chill.

LEMON DRESSING

INGREDIENTS:
- 1 tsp minced garlic (*1 clove*)
- 2 Tbsps. lemon juice
- ¼ tsp sea salt
- ¼ tsp cayenne pepper (*optional*)
- 3 Tbsps. extra-virgin olive oil
- 2 Tbsps. raw honey or maple syrup

DIRECTIONS:
1. Finely mince a clove of garlic.
2. In a salad dressing jar place lemon juice, cayenne pepper and salt.
3. Whisk to combine all ingredients.
4. Slowly pour extra-virgin olive oil, whisking as you go to incorporate.
5. Taste to check seasoning and it is done. Enjoy it on your favorite salad.

STRING BEANS with ALMONDS or CASHEW NUTS

INGREDIENTS:
- 2 cups string beans
- ½ cup raw almonds or cashew nuts soaked overnight and drain
- 1 ½ Tbsps. coconut or olive oil
- Sea salt to taste
- 1 small onion chopped
- 2 garlic cloves chopped
- 1 tsp basil leaves
- 1 tsp parsley leaves dried or fresh
- 1 sprig celery minced or dash celery salt

DIRECTION:
1. Clean and wash string beans, cut into bite sized pieces.
2. Remove the skin from almonds and cut each into two or three pieces.
3. Add oil to hot pan, mix in onions, garlic, and tomato and let stir fry for a minute.
4. Add string beans and nuts and then remaining dry ingredients.
5. Add a small amount of water or coconut milk and let cook for 2 minutes.

FRESH PAPAYA SALSA

INGREDIENTS:
- 3 cups diced fresh papaya
- 2 cups cherry tomatoes halved *(optional)*
- ½ cup chopped cilantro
- 3–4 green onions thinly sliced into rounds
- 1 jalapeno pepper seeded and finely diced
- 1–2 limes juiced
- Dash extra virgin olive oil
- ½ tsp sea salt

DIRECTIONS:
1. Toss all ingredients together in a bowl. Let sit for about 10 minutes before serving to let the flavors mingle.

EASY SESAME CABBAGE SLAW

INGREDIENTS:
- 1 cabbage head shredded *(lightly steamed and cooled)*
- ¼ cup red onion minced
- ⅓ cup unsweetened natural peanut or almond butter
- ¼ cup lemon juice
- 1–2 Tbsps. fresh ginger minced
- 1 garlic clove minced
- 2 Tbsps. sesame seeds toasted
- Dash sea salt
- ¼ tsp paprika
- 1 Tbsp. raw honey or maple syrup

DIRECTIONS:
1. In large bowl, toss the cabbage and onion.
2. In smaller bowl, mix the remaining ingredients, whisking until the peanut or almond butter is completely dissolved.
3. Toss the dressing with the cabbage mixture, and refrigerate for 30–60 minutes, or until you're ready to serve.

CREAMY CASHEW MAYONNAISE

INGREDIENTS:
- 2 cups warm water
- ½ cup cashews
- 2 Tbsps. lemon juice
- 1 Tbsp. onion powder or one small onion
- 1 tsp. garlic powder or two garlic gloves
- ½ tsp. sea salt
- 1 tsp. maple syrup or raw honey
- 1 tsp. arrowroot powder (*optional*)
- Herbs (dill, basil, parsley, oregano, cayenne, turmeric etc.) to create herbal cashew mayo (**Optional**)

DIRECTIONS:
1. Blend all ingredients until smooth. Bring to a gentle boil in a sauce pot over medium heat.
2. Maintain a constant stir until thickened. Stir in lemon juice last and allow to cool.

HOMEMADE TOMATO KETCHUP

INGREDIENTS:
- 1 cup unsalted tomato sauce or 1 cup sundried tomatoes
- 4 tsps. raw honey
- ¼ tsp sea salt
- ½ tsp onion salt
- ¼ tsp garlic powder
- ¼ tsp onion powder
- ¼ tsp coriander and cardamom
- 1/8 tsp celery salt
- 1 ½ tsps. lemon juice
- ½ tsp molasses

DIRECTIONS:
1. Pour all ingredients in a blender. Blend until smooth.
2. Let sit on counter approximately 1 hour, then refrigerate. Will last in fridge for 6–7 days.

HOMEMADE CURRY POWDER

INGREDIENTS:
- 2 Tbsps. coriander powder
- 1 ½ tsps. fenugreek seeds
- 2 tsps. turmeric powder
- 1 tsp celery seeds
- 1 tsp onion powder
- 1 tsp garlic powder
- 6 bay leaves
- ½ tsp paprika
- ½ tsp cumin

DIRECTIONS:
1. Grind all ingredients to powder in a blender. Store in a bottle container in kitchen cupboard.

CINNAMON SUBSTITUTE

INGREDIENTS:
- 1 Tbsp. coriander
- 1 Tbsp. Bay leaf
- 1 Tbsp. cardamom

DIRECTIONS:
1. Put all ingredients in a blender and blend until properly combined. Bottle and label.

Soups

8 Recipes

BROAD BEAN and CARROT SOUP

INGREDIENTS:
- 1 cup broad or butter beans cooked
- 1 onion chopped
- 2 large carrots chopped
- 1 celery stalk
- 1 scallion stalk
- 1 cup pure water
- 1 cup of coconut milk
- ½ tsp sea salt
- ½ tsp turmeric powder
- Bash basil and marjoram herbs
- Bash cayenne pepper to taste (*optional*)
- 2 cloves garlic chopped finely
- Sprig of fresh thyme
- 2 Tbsps. cold pressed coconut oil

DIRECTIONS:
1. In a heated Soup pot pour in coconut oil and add onions, garlic and scallion. Cook until soft for 1 minute.
2. Add in celery and carrots, cover with water and coconut milk.
3. Bring to a boil and let simmer for 2 minutes just to soften the vegetables.
4. Carefully pour all the ingredients into blender and pulse to the smooth consistency that you like (*some like ruff chopped soup, others smooth and creamy*).
5. Pour mixture back into the pot and add thyme, basil, marjoram, broad beans, turmeric, salt, and pepper.
6. Let the soup come to a boil and allow to simmer for another 10 minutes.
7. Turn off the stove and allow to cool. Sprinkle fresh chopped parsley on top and enjoy!

BLACK BEAN SOUP

INGREDIENTS:
- 2 cups cooked black beans (*soaked overnight and cooked on medium heat for 1 hour the next day in fresh water*)
- 3 cups water
- 2 small tomatoes
- 1 medium onion peeled
- 3 cloves garlic
- ½ red pepper seeded
- 2 scallion stalks cleaned and trimmed
- 2 Tbsps. cold pressed coconut or olive oil
- ½ tsp cumin seed powder
- 2 medium carrots diced
- 1 pumpkin sliced and diced
- 2 tsps. Thyme leaves
- ½ tsp sea salt

DIRECTIONS:
1. In a soup pot, sauté onion, garlic, and scallion in oil for 2–3 minutes.
2. Add remaining ingredients and cook for 10–15 minutes. Add salt and pepper to taste.
3. Carefully pour the hot soup in a bowl and serve.

PUMPKIN SOUP with COCONUT MILK

INGREDIENTS:
- 2 pounds pumpkin (*or a larger amount depending on your taste*)
- 1 red onion chopped
- 2 celery stalks chopped
- 2 sweet potatoes peeled and chopped
- 3 garlic cloves peeled and chopped
- 1–inch fresh ginger peeled and grated
- 2 small carrots
- 2 tsps. sea salt
- 1 tsp ground turmeric
- ¼ tsp ground cumin
- ¼ tsp ground cardamom
- 4 cups vegetable broth or pure water
- 2 cups coconut milk
- 2 scallion stalks
- Sprig of thyme

DIRECTIONS:
1. Place pumpkin, all vegetables, salt and spices into the soup pot.
2. Pour in water or vegetable broth and coconut milk and stir mixture. Cover and cook on low for 30 minutes.
3. Use blender to puree the pumpkin into chunks or blend until smooth. Season with more salt as desired.
4. Add scallion, thyme, onions or whatever your taste desires. Cook for another 15 minutes. Enjoy!

MIXED VEGETABLE SOUP

INGREDIENTS:

- 1 small onion chopped
- 2 cloves garlic
- 2 tsps. fresh thyme
- 2 medium sized carrots diced
- ½ cup spinach
- ½ cup turnip diced
- ½ cup Pinto Beans cooked
- ¼ cup chopped cabbage
- 3 cups coconut milk or plain water
- 2 pinches garlic and onion powder
- ½ tsp cumin seeds powder
- ½ coriander seeds powder
- Coriander leaves (*few*)
- Sea salt to taste

DIRECTIONS:

1. Combine onions, scallion, thyme, and garlic cloves in pot. Add coconut milk or water, beans, and vegetables.
2. Add a little sea salt to contents. Boil mixture on low flame for 20 minutes until contents become soft and cooked.
3. Put the cooked content into a soup processor or blender and blend until chunky or smooth.
4. Add powdered spices and other seasonings. Boil for about 5 minutes. Garnish with coriander leaves or parley, as desired.

CHICKPEAS and VEGETABLE SOUP

INGREDIENTS:
- 3 cups pure water
- 4 cloves garlic chopped
- 1 large, sweet potato peeled and diced
- 1 large carrot diced
- 1 small turnip diced
- 1 yellow bell pepper seeded, cored, and diced
- 2 scallion stalks
- 2 Tbsps. fresh thyme
- 3 medium tomatoes diced
- 4 cups chickpeas cooked
- 2 cups coconut milk
- 1 lime juiced
- 1 Tbsp. turmeric powder
- Pinch cumin and coriander powder
- 2 cups of pumpkin chopped
- Sea salt to taste

Add just before serving (optional):
- 1–2 Tbsps. fresh cilantro or mint chopped
- 1 cup packed baby greens

DIRECTIONS:
1. Combine all ingredients in a slow cooker and cook until tender.
2. If you're in a more hands-on mood, do it the rolled way. Throw everything in a pot and cook, covered, over medium heat until the vegetables are tender for about thirty (30) minutes.
3. Stir in cilantro or mint and baby greens. Heat through briefly until the greens soften and serve.

CALLALOO and SPINACH COCONUT SOUP

INGREDIENTS:
- ½ bundle chopped callaloo (*don't throw away seeds; put them in soup also*)
- 1 cup spinach chopped
- 2 cups coconut milk
- 1 cup cooked lentils
- 1 Tbsp. turmeric powder or grated turmeric
- ½ tsp. sea salt
- 2 garlic cloves thinly sliced
- Pinch grated ginger
- Handful parsley and celery
- Pinch cayenne pepper
- 2 Tbsps. coconut oil
- 1 small onion diced
- 2 scallion stalks chopped
- ¼ tsp. fresh thyme leave
- ⅛ tsp. dried basil
- Herbs of your liking: sage, oregano, cumin
- Juice of quarter lime

DIRECTIONS:
1. Wash callaloo and spinach properly and cut into small pieces. In a medium sized soup pot place coconut oil, garlic, scallion, cooked lentils, onion, and ginger. Allow to cook until soften for 1 minute. Add coconut milk.
2. Bring to a boil and add callaloo, spinach, cayenne pepper, basil, thyme, turmeric, other herbs and salt.
3. Let simmer for 10 minutes, turn off stove and let sit for about 5 minutes.
   NB: If you can find some fresh moringa leaves add it to the soup after you have turned the stove off – this will increase the nutrients even more and help with your recovery from the virus.
4. Enjoy soup by itself or serve with fresh salad (*have salad first and then soup with some homemade bread*). Squeeze lime juice into soup, when you are just about to have your meal.

LENTILS and CARROT SOUP

INGREDIENTS:
- 2 Tbsps. olive oil
- 2 onions chopped
- ½ tsp. sea salt
- 6 cloves garlic minced
- 1 cup tomatoes diced
- 3 stalks scallion
- 1 spring thyme
- 1 ½ cups Lentil
- ½ cup turnip washed and diced
- 3 cups pure water
- 2 cups coconut milk
- 2 cups sweet potato peeled and cubed
- 1 tsp. oregano
- 4 tsps. cumin
- ¼ tsp. cayenne pepper (*optional*)
- ½ tsp. sage powder
- 2 bay leaves
- 3 cups carrots (*about 6–8 carrots*) sliced in half lengthwise then in 1/4-inch slices
- 1 ½ cups celery (*about 6 ribs*) sliced in half lengthwise then in 1/4-inch slices

DIRECTIONS:
1. Heat olive oil in large, heavy bottomed Dutch oven. Add onions and salt and sauté for 2 minutes or until tender and translucent. Add garlic, scallion and tomatoes, stirring often for about 1–2 minutes. (*The goal is to let tomatoes brown or caramelize a little on the bottom of the pan without burning*).
2. Add half the water and coconut milk and scrape the bottom of the pan to deglaze.
3. Add rest of water along with potatoes, turnip, lentils, thyme, scallion, oregano, cumin, pepper, salt, and bay leaves. Bring to a boil then reduce to simmer.
4. Cover and simmer for about 25 minutes or until lentils are just about cooked all the way through.
5. Add carrots and celery last. Cover and simmer another 10 minutes or so or until vegetables and lentils are tender and soup is thickened. Remove bay leaves and serve. *This soup tastes even better the next day for leftovers*.

LENTIL and SWEET POTATO SOUP

INGREDIENTS:
- 1 Tbsp. extra-virgin olive oil
- 1 medium onion chopped
- 1 Tbsp. arrowroot powder (*thickening agent*)
- 4 garlic cloves minced
- Salt to taste
- 2 tsps. cumin seeds lightly toasted and ground
- 2 medium carrots diced
- ¼ cup diced pumpkin
- 1 ½ cups brown or green lentils rinsed
- 4 stalks scallion washed and chopped
- 4 cups water
- 2 cups coconut milk
- 2 medium-size sweet potatoes peeled and cut in large dice
- 1 tsp sage
- 2 small tomatoes diced
- ¼ cup diced red or yellow bell pepper
- 1 bay leaf
- ¼ cup chopped fresh cilantro or parsley to taste
- Dash of cayenne pepper
- 1 tsp turmeric powder
- Lime wedges for serving

DIRECTIONS:
1. Heat olive oil over medium heat in a large, heavy soup pot or Dutch oven and add onion, scallion, and garlic.
2. Cook, stirring often, until it softens, about 2 minutes, and add bell pepper and salt.
3. Cook, stirring, until garlic smells fragrant, about 30 seconds, and add ground cumin seeds and carrots.
4. Stir together for a minute, then add lentils, water, sweet potatoes, tomatoes, turmeric powder, sage, pumpkin, coconut milk, salt and bay leaf.

5. Bring to a boil, reduce heat, cover and simmer 40–45 minutes, until lentils and sweet potatoes are tender and the broth fragrant. Taste and adjust seasoning, you can add a dash of cayenne pepper if you desire.
6. Stir in cilantro or parsley, simmer for another minute.
7. *Serve, passing lime wedges to diners so they can season their lentils with a squeeze of lime juice if desired*.

Sauces

5 Recipes

SWEET POTATO SALAD in COCONUT CREAM SAUCE

INGREDIENTS:
- 1 lb. sweet potatoes (*about 2 medium*), preferably organic, peeled and chopped into 1" pieces
- ½ cup coconut cream
- 2 Tbsps. mango chutney
- 1 tsp turmeric powder
- ¼ cup organic raisins
- ¼ cup green onions chopped plus more for garnish
- Sea salt to taste

DIRECTIONS:
1. Place cubed potatoes in a medium saucepan, cover with cold water, and bring to a boil over high heat.
2. Cook until the potatoes are tender but not mushy for about 10–15 minutes. Drain cooked potatoes.
3. **Coconut cream sauce**: Mix coconut cream, mango chutney, turmeric, organic raisins, and salt in a bowl.
4. While potatoes are draining, stir together the remaining ingredients in a large bowl.
5. While the potatoes are still warm, add them to the coconut cream sauce and stir gently to evenly coat the potatoes. Garnish with green onions
6. Chill in the refrigerator (*preferably overnight*) to allow flavors to come together.

CHERRY NASEBERRY ALMOND SAUCE

INGREDIENTS:
- 1 ½ cups cherries juiced
- ½ cup almonds
- 1 medium naseberry
- 2–4 Tbsps. raw honey
- ½ tsp. coriander powder
- ½ tsp. sea salt
- ¼ cup organic raisins

DIRECTIONS:
1. Put all ingredients in a blender and blend until combined and smooth. You can make this a sauce for porridge, to pour over fruits or cereal.
2. May use as a dip for your home–made bread or flaxseed crackers.
3. You can warm the sauce and serve with your home-made veggie burgers or nut loaf.

CHICKPEAS and SWEET POTATO in CASHEW CREAM SAUCE

INGREDIENTS:
- 2 cups cooked chickpeas (*soak overnight and cook in fresh water for 2 hours the next morning*)
- 1 cup coconut milk
- ¼ cup raw cashew nuts
- 2 cups cubed peeled sweet potato
- ½ tsp sea salt
- ¼ tsp each: sage, oregano, marjoram, basil and parsley, herbs
- 1 large onion diced
- 3 stalks scallion diced
- ½ red or yellow bell pepper diced
- Sprig of fresh thyme
- 1 Tbsp. turmeric powder
- 1 tsp arrow root powder (*to thicken stew*)
- Dash of cayenne pepper to taste

DIRECTIONS:
1. When chickpeas are almost cooked add sweet potato to pot and finish cooking for about 20 minutes.
2. When peas and potato are finished cooking, pour off water and put pot on stove at medium heat.
3. In blender add coconut milk and cashews. Blend until smooth and pour into pot.
4. Add arrow root powder, seasonings, herbs and spices, then let cook for 25–30 minutes on low heat.
5. Enjoy with brown rice, steamed and raw vegetables, or favorite ground provision: yam, pumpkin, or dasheen.

CASHEW SUNFLOWER SEED SAUCE

INGREDIENTS:
- ¼ cup cashew
- ¼ cup sunflower seeds
- ½ cup water
- ½ tsp turmeric
- Onion, scallion, garlic, sage, red bell pepper, basil
- Salt to taste

DIRECTIONS:
1. Blend cashew and sunflower seeds with water until smooth and creamy.
2. Pour into a sauce pot over medium heat and bring to a boil. Add spices, salt, and herbs.
3. Simmer for 10 minutes. Turn off stove, pour into blender and blend until creamy.
4. Put back on stove over low heat and let simmer for another 10 minutes. Serve with Lentil Balls.

LENTIL BALLS with CASHEW and SUNFLOWER SEED SAUCE

INGREDIENTS:
- 1 ½ cups lentils
- 2 ½ cups pure water
- 1 cup spelt flour
- 2 Tbsps. grounded flaxseeds
- 1 small onion diced
- 3 stalks scallion
- 3 cloves garlic
- 1 tsp sea salt (*or to your taste*)
- ½ cup grated coconut
- Herbs: parsley, sage, basil, dash of cayenne pepper (*optional*)
- 3 Tbsps. virgin coconut oil
- ¼ cup rolled oats flour (*grounded*)
- 2 small tomatoes diced

DIRECTIONS:
1. Cook lentils in two cups of water for 20 minutes or until tender.
2. In a bowl add all ingredients, mix well with a large spoon, then scoop out tablespoon amounts and roll into balls in the middle of your hands. Place them on parchment paper on a baking sheet.
3. Bake at 325°F for 45–50 minutes or until golden brown and firm to the touch.

Stews, Stir Fry, Balls, Steamed Dishes

33 Recipes

SWEET POTATO and LENTIL STEW

INGREDIENTS:
- ½ cup brown lentils
- 1 onion finely chopped
- 2 scallion stalks
- ½ cup coconut milk
- 1 cup pure water
- 3 Tbsps. olive oil
- 3 garlic cloves minced
- 1 tsp. ground cumin
- ½ tsp. ground turmeric
- 1 tsp. paprika
- 1 medium tomato finely chopped
- 1 tsp. molasses or raw honey
- 1 tsp. sea salt to taste
- 2 sweet potatoes peeled and cut into 1" cubes
- 1 lemon grated zest
- 4 Tbsps. flat–leaf parsley finely chopped
- ¼ cup organic raisins (optional)

DIRECTIONS:
1. Rinse the lentils in a sieve. Place in a pot with onion and water.
2. Cover and bring to a simmer over low heat. Cook for 15 minutes. Pour off water and add in coconut milk.
3. In a small nonstick frying pan, heat the oil over low heat. Add garlic, sauté for 15 seconds, then add cumin, turmeric, paprika, scallion, tomato and honey or molasses, and cook, stirring constantly, for 2 minutes until it forms a dark, aromatic paste.
4. Add spice paste to lentils, along with salt. After lentils have been cooked for 10 minutes with the spices and herbs, add the sweet potatoes, plus an additional half cup of water.
5. Let cook for 15 minutes, stirring occasionally to keep the potatoes from sticking.
6. Add lemon zest and half the parsley. Cook until lentils and sweet potatoes are done (*add more water if necessary*). Taste and adjust seasoning with lemon juice, honey and salt as needed. Add in the organic raisins and turn off the stove. Garnish with remaining parsley. Serve over couscous, brown rice, quinoa or steamed millet.

LENTILS and STEW

INGREDIENTS:
- 2 Tbsps. olive or coconut oil
- 1 small onion diced
- ½ cup diced red or yellow bell pepper
- ¼ tsp cayenne pepper
- 2 cloves garlic minced
- 2 stalks scallion diced
- 1 cup cooked lentils
- ½ cup coconut milk
- 1 tsp. turmeric powder
- ¼ tsp sage
- ¼ tsp cumin
- Sea salt to taste
- 1 cup ackee picked and cleaned

DIRECTIONS:
1. In a stainless-steel pot, sauté onion, scallion and garlic in coconut oil until translucent, add cooked lentils and all other herbs. Add coconut milk and bring to a boil, then add salt.
2. Reduce heat to low, add washed uncooked ackee, cover and simmer for 20 minutes or until ackee is soft and cooked. Serve hot with spelt flour dumplings, yam, pumpkin, brown rice.

THREE BEAN or PEAS STEW

INGREDIENTS:
- 1 cup broad beans
- 1 cup (*Pigeon*) Gungo peas
- 1 cup chickpeas
- 1 cup coconut milk
- 2 medium carrots
- Small pumpkin piece cut in small cubes
- 2 tsps. pepper powder, garlic powder and onion powder
- 1 tsp cumin seeds powder
- ½ tsp coriander seeds powder
- Few coriander leaves
- Rock salt to taste
- 3 Tbsps. cold pressed coconut or olive oil
- 1 tsp basil leaves and parsley leaves
- 3 Tbsps. turmeric powder
- Onion, garlic cloves, scallion, thyme, green and red sweet pepper

DIRECTION:
1. Soak peas and beans overnight. Throw away water the next day and put in a pot to boil with fresh water for 1 hour or until tender.
2. In a heated saucepan pour oil and combine chopped onions, scallion, thyme and garlic cloves.
3. Add turmeric and remaining dry ingredients.
4. Add a little sea salt and coconut milk to the contents with the carrots and diced pumpkin.
5. Boil the mixture on a low flame for five (5) minutes.
6. Add the cooked beans and let simmer for another ten (10) minutes until cooked.

SPLIT PEAS and LENTIL STEW served with QUINOA and CALLALOO

INGREDIENTS:
- 1 cup split peas cooked
- 1 cup lentils cooked
- 1 large onion diced
- 1 large carrot diced
- 2 medium Irish potatoes diced
- 1 cup coconut milk
- ½ tsp sea salt
- 1 tsp turmeric powder
- Herbs: scallion, parsley, cumin, garlic, coriander, basil, ginger, marjoram, oregano, cayenne, thyme

DIRECTIONS:
1. Over medium heat in a pot, sauté onion, garlic, scallion using only two tablespoons of water or coconut oil.
2. Add in diced carrots, potatoes, and coconut milk. Allow to come to a boil, and then add in salt, herbs, turmeric, lentils, and split peas.
3. Simmer on low heat for about 25–30 minutes.

QUINOA and CALLALOO

INGREDIENTS:
- ½ cup quinoa
- 1 cup pure water
- ¼ tsp sea salt
- 2 cups of shredded callaloo

DIRECTIONS:
1. Bring water to boil. Add in salt and quinoa.
2. Turn stove down to low heat and cook until quinoa is light and fluffy for about 20 minutes.
3. Once the quinoa is cooked, add in the callaloo (*that you have thoroughly washed*) and let steam for another 3 minutes. Serve with Split Peas and Lentil Stew for breakfast or lunch.

STEWED DRIED GUNGO PEAS STEW

INGREDIENTS:
- 2 cups dried Gungo (*Pigeon or Congo*) peas cooked
- 2 scallion stalks
- 1 Tbsps. olive or coconut oil
- 1 medium tomato diced
- 1 cup bell pepper diced
- 1 scotch bonnet pepper (*keep whole for flavor*)
- 1 medium onion diced
- 2 garlic cloves
- 3 sprigs thyme
- 1 Tbsp. parsley
- ½ cup celery diced
- ¼ tsp sea salt
- ¾ cup coconut milk
- ½ cup water
- 1 tsp turmeric powder
- ¼ tsp each: sage, oregano, and basil (*dried herbs*)
- 1 Tbsp. arrow root powder (*thickening agent for gravy*)

Optional: grated ginger, diced carrots, pumpkin, sweet potato

DIRECTIONS:
1. Put a little water in pot (*stainless steel or ceramic*) at medium flame. Add celery, garlic, tomato, parsley, thyme, onion and scallions. Turn the heat down to low and let it gently cook for about 2 minutes.
2. Drain and rinse the dried Gungo peas that you have cooked overnight. Turn the heat up to med or high.
3. Add the remaining ingredients and bring to a boil. Reduce to a simmer and let cook for about 15 minutes.
4. Taste for salt and adjust at this point.
5. Add some diced Irish potato, sweet potato or diced pumpkin when adding the peas to pot to achieve additional body to stew dish or just to stretch it a bit if you desire. Add more liquid and salt as desired.
6. Add the coconut oil last after the stew is cooked.
7. Serve with steamed brown rice, Roasted Breadfruit, boiled green bananas, home-made flax or pumpkin bread or what is available.

GUNGO PEAS and TOFU COCONUT STEW

INGREDIENTS:
- 1 pack/bar Organic Non-GMO firm Tofu
- 1 cup green Gungo Peas (*Pigeon peas*)
- ½ cup coconut milk
- 2 Tbsps. cold pressed coconut oil
- Dried Herbs: cumin, oregano, sage, basil, cayenne pepper (*a dash of each*)
- 1 medium onion chopped
- 2 scallion stalks chopped
- 2 cloves garlic crushed
- 1 sprig fresh thyme
- ½ medium red bell pepper cut in strips
- ½ tsp. Himalayan or Celtic Sea salt
- 1 tsp. turmeric powder
- 1 Tbsp. arrowroot powder or breadfruit flour (*thickening agent for gravy*)
- 1 Tbsp. honey

DIRECTIONS:
1. Boil Gungo Peas for 10 minutes or until cooked, then drain off water.
2. Put cooking pot (*stainless steel, glass or ceramic pots and pans*) on stove at medium heat and add the oil.
3. Cut Tofu into strips and add to the very hot pot (*if pot is not very hot Tofu will stick and break up into pieces*).
4. Stir fry for about 3 minutes until golden. Add onion, scallion, garlic, thyme and turmeric and stir fry for 1 minute. Add coconut milk, cooked Gungo Peas and all dried herbs, salt, bell pepper strips, honey and arrowroot powder. Allow to simmer at low heat for 10 minutes, then turn stove off.

This vegetarian protein dish can be served with steamed brown rice, yam, boiled bananas or plantain, roasted breadfruit, Quinoa or baked Irish or sweet potatoes.

LENTILS and GUNGO STEW

INGREDIENTS:
- 2 Tbsps. olive or coconut oil
- 1 small onion diced
- 2 cloves garlic minced
- 2 scallion stalks diced
- 1 cup diced tomatoes
- 1 cup cooked Lentils
- 1 cup cooked Gungo peas
- 1 cup coconut milk
- 1 bay leaf
- 1 tsp turmeric powder
- ¼ tsp sage
- ¼ tsp cumin
- Sea salt to taste
- 1 cup string beans chopped
- Other herbs: parsley, basil, dill

DIRECTIONS:
1. In a stainless-steel pot, sauté scallion, onion, and garlic in olive oil until translucent.
2. Add cooked Lentils, Gungo peas, coconut milk, bay leaf, turmeric, sage, cumin, and salt.
3. Bring to a slow boil, reduce heat to low, cover and simmer for 20 minutes.
4. Add remaining herbs, string beans, tomatoes and red bell pepper and let simmer for another 5 minutes.
5. Serve with steamed brown rice and plantain, avocado, tomatoes, and cucumber.

LENTILS, RIPE PLANTAIN and STRING BEAN STEW

INGREDIENTS:
- 2 Tbsp. olive or coconut oil or water
- 1 small onion diced
- 2 cloves garlic minced
- 1 cup string beans diced
- 2 scallion stalks diced
- 1 cup cooked Lentils
- ½ cup coconut milk or water
- 1 bay leaf
- 1 tsp turmeric powder
- ¼ teaspoon herbs: sage, cumin, basil, coriander, thyme
- Sea salt to taste
- 1 cup diced ripe plantain

DIRECTIONS:
1. In a stainless-steel pot on medium heat, sauté onion and garlic in olive or coconut oil (or water) until translucent, then add scallion and stir.
2. Add cooked lentils, coconut milk, bay leaf, turmeric, basil, thyme, sage, coriander, cumin, and salt.
3. Bring to a slow boil, reduce heat to low, cover and simmer for 15 minutes or until lentils, spices and herbs are all combined and soft.
4. Add ripe plantain and spring beans last and let simmer for another 3 minutes.
   Serve with brown rice or steamed yam, baked potatoes with cucumber, pumpkin, tomatoes, homemade biscuits or bread.

KIDNEY BEAN STEW

INGREDIENTS:
- 3 cups cooked kidney beans
- 3 stalks scallions chopped
- 1 large onion diced
- 2 sprigs thyme
- 1 Tbsp. parsley
- 1 Tbsp. olive oil
- 1 medium tomato diced
- Herbs: sage, basil, coriander, cumin, cayenne pepper
- 1 scotch bonnet pepper (*optional*)
- 2 cups coconut milk
- 4 cloves garlic
- ½ cup red or yellow bell pepper
- -½ cup diced carrots
- ½ cup diced pumpkin
- 1 tsp grated ginger
- 1 Tbsp. arrow root powder (*thickening agent*)
- 1 tsp sea salt to taste

DIRECTIONS:
1. Chop (onion, scallion, and parsley), dice (tomato, bell pepper), crush (garlic) and remove thyme leaves from springs. Heat oil on medium flame in a deep saucepan, and then add garlic, onion, bell pepper, scallion, thyme and parsley. Lower heat to its lowest and let it go for about 4–5 minutes. *Here's where we'll get an infusion of flavors.* **The scotch bonnet pepper is only for flavor, and should not be cut open, but put in whole and removed once stew is cooked.**
2. Add all other ingredients, coconut milk and kidney beans. Put lid on pot (*still on low heat*) and bring to a boil.
3. Reduce to simmer and cook for about 30 minutes. For a thicker gravy, use back of spoon and crush some of beans.

CURRIED LIMA BEAN STEW

INGREDIENTS:
- 4 cups boiled Lima beans (*also called butter beans*)
- 2 Tbsps. coconut oil
- 1 Tbsp. turmeric powder
- ½ tsp paprika
- 2 fresh tomatoes diced
- 1 Tbsp. molasses
- ½ cup coconut milk
- ½ tsp cumin powder
- ¼ tsp sage
- 1 sprigs fresh thyme
- ½ tsp sea salt to taste
- ½ medium purple onion diced
- 3 stalks scallion diced
- 2 cloves garlic minced
- ½ red bell pepper diced

DIRECTIONS:
1. Put Lima beans to soak for a minimum of 6 hours, throw off water, then boil in a pot for 45 minutes to 1 hour. Heat coconut oil in a pan. Add turmeric, paprika, onions, scallion, and minced garlic.
2. Let herbs and spices roast in oil for about 30 seconds. Then pour in coconut milk.
3. Allow to come to a boil for a few minutes. Add cooked Lima beans, thyme, sage, cumin, tomatoes, and bell pepper. Let simmer for about 5 minutes or until liquid is reduced. Stir and leave to cook for another 3 minutes.
4. You may adjust sauce consistency by adding one tablespoon of arrowroot powder to thicken it.
5. Add molasses and salt last. Leave to simmer for another 15 minutes, give everything a good stir, and turn off heat.

SPROUTED LENTIL COCONUT STEW

INGREDIENTS:
- 1 cup sprouted lentils
- 2 tsps. Parsley
- 2 stalks scallion
- 1 medium onion
- ¼ cup coconut cream or milk
- Salt to taste
- ¼ cup shredded carrots
- 1 sprig of thyme
- Dash of coriander powder
- 1 tsp. Turmeric powder
- 1 Tbsp. coconut oil
- ½ tsp. cilantro

DIRECTIONS:
1. Chop all vegetables and herbs into small pieces.
2. In a medium stainless steel or glass cooking pot, using coconut oil, sauté all ingredients except sprouts.
3. After 1 minute add coconut cream, then sprouts. Allow simmer at low heat for 10 minutes.
4. Serve with vegetable salad and enjoy.

(Regular dried lentils are rich in protein but does not contain adequate amounts of all the 9 essential amino acids. They only contain small amounts of methionine and thus are not regarded as a complete protein. Sprouted lentils, on the other hand, contain increased amounts of all nine essential amino acids, thus a complete protein food).

HOW TO SPROUT SEEDS:
1. Allow dried whole seeds to soak in fresh water over night.
2. Next morning throw off water. Place seeds into a strainer or sieve to about ¼ or ½ way to the top.
3. Rest strainer in a container ensuring it is not touching the bottom of the container.

4. Use a dark lip or a kitchen towel to cover strainer.
5. Every 8 hours (*or there about*) pour water on seeds, the excess water will drain into the container, and you will discard this.
6. By day two you will start to see the sprouting started (*as seed is starting to grow into a little plant*). Sprouts are ready to harvest and be consumed when they are about ½ to 1 inch in length.

VEGETARIAN CURRIED GUNGO (Pigeon) PEAS

INGREDIENTS:
- 3 cups green Gungo (pigeon) peas shelled
- ½ tsp sea salt
- ¼ tsp cayenne pepper
- ½ medium onion diced
- 4 cloves garlic crushed
- 2 stalks scallion, diced
- 2 Tbsps. virgin coconut oil
- ¼ scotch bonnet pepper (remain whole for flavor)
- 1 Tbsp. turmeric powder
- Herbs: parsley, basil, oregano, marjoram
- ½ tsp sage powder
- ½ small red bell pepper diced
- 1 small Tania (*called coco in Jamaica*) or Irish potato
- 2 cups coconut milk or plain water
- 1 bay leaf

DIRECTIONS:
1. Heat oil in a deep saucepan on medium heat. Add diced onion, scallion and garlic, turn heat to low and cook for 3 minutes. With heat still on low, add turmeric, sage and stir well. Let that toast for about 1 minute.
2. Add cayenne pepper and give it a quick stir. Rinse and drain green pigeon peas then add to pot at this point.
3. Turn up heat, add coconut milk (or water), diced coco or Irish potato, salt, red bell pepper and all other herbs.
4. Bring to boil, then reduce to simmer and cook for about 35–40 minutes with lid slightly ajar. Stir occasionally.
5. Gravy will start to thicken. If still thin, use back of spoon to crush some of the cooked peas to help thicken gravy. Taste for salt and adjust accordingly. You

can also turn up the heat to burn off any extra liquid. This is an excellent side for roti, brown rice, breadfruit, quinoa, or homemade bread.

LIMA BEAN, CARROT and PUMPKIN STEW

INGREDIENTS:
- 2 cups lima beans
- 1 cup diced carrots
- 1 cup diced pumpkin
- 2 cups coconut milk
- 2 Tbsps. virgin coconut oil
- 1 Tbsp. sea salt to taste
- Herbs: sage, cayenne, basil, parsley, garlic
- 1 tsp turmeric powder
- 1 small onion diced
- 3 stalks scallion
- 1 sprig thyme

DIRECTIONS:
1. Cook lima beans in three cups of water until tender, if you soak overnight, cooking time will be approximately 1 hour, cooking on medium heat.
2. In a pot, over medium heat add oil, onions, garlic, and scallion. Cook for 1 minute, then add cooked lima beans and coconut milk. Add all herbs, turmeric powder and salt. Bring to a boil then reduce heat.
3. Cook for 20 minutes then add carrots and pumpkin. Add arrow root powder to thicken gravy.
4. Let simmer for another 20 minutes until carrot and pumpkin are cooked and there is a nice gravy consistency. Enjoy with brown rice, roasted breadfruit, quinoa, yam or sweet potato.

LIMA BEAN STEW with ACKEE

Sometimes called "butter beans" because of their starchy yet buttery texture, lima beans have a delicate flavor that complements a wide variety of dishes.

INGREDIENTS:
- 1 cup of cooked lima beans
- 1 medium onion
- 3 stalks scallion
- 2 cloves garlic
- ½ cup coconut milk
- ½ tsp. sea salt
- Herbs: sage, basil, garlic, turmeric, marjoram
- 1 cup ackee washed and properly picked

DIRECTIONS:
1. Place herbs and seasonings in pot with coconut milk. Bring to a boil then add cooked Lima beans.
2. Cook for 15–20 minutes, then add ackees and cook for another 15 minutes on low heat. Add salt to taste last.

KALE, CALLALOO and PEANUT CHOWDER

INGREDIENTS:
- 1 purple or yellow onion diced
- ¼ cup peanut roasted or raw
- 4 cloves garlic
- 2 Tbsps. coconut oil
- ½ tsp grated ginger
- 1 tsp. turmeric powder
- 1 medium carrot chopped
- 1 medium carrot grated
- 1 heaping Tbsp. dried parsley
- ½ dried oregano
- 1 cup vegetable stock or water
- 2 Tbsps. sesame seeds
- 2 cups coconut milk
- 3 stalks scallion
- 3 stalks callaloo, stripped and cut into small pieces
- 3 cups kale, de-stemmed, finely chopped
- ½ tsp. sea salt to taste

DIRECTIONS:
1. Sauté onions, scallion and garlic in coconut or olive oil for about 2 minutes. Stirring.
2. Add sesame seeds and peanut. Add vegetable stock, coconut milk and chopped carrots, then bring to a boil.
3. Place most of soup into a blender. Add all pieces of chopped carrot in blender. Process until smooth and then place back in pot.
4. Add ginger, grated carrots, chopped kale, callaloo, turmeric and sea salt.
5. Simmer another 5–6 minutes until kale and callaloo are thoroughly cooked.
6. Serves 3 as an entree, 5 as a side dish.

VEGAN KIDNEY BEAN CHILLI

INGREDIENTS:
- 1 Tbsp. cayenne powder
- 2 Tbsps. cumin powder
- ½ tsp. red pepper
- 2 cloves garlic
- 1 medium onion chopped
- 3 scallion stalks chopped
- 2 Tbsps. sweet pepper diced
- 1 Tbsp. dried or fresh thyme
- 1 Tbsp. basil leaves
- 32 oz. tomatoes diced
- 1 cup water or coconut milk
- 3 cups of red kidney beans (*soak overnight – drain and add fresh water and cook until beans are tender*)

DIRECTIONS:
1. In large sauce pan cook onions (*add a little water so it does not get crispy*) with garlic, sweet pepper and scallion until they are soft.
2. Add other ingredients (*except cayenne pepper which is optional*) to pan. If you want a soupier chili, add some extra water until you get the consistency you desire.
3. Cook for about twenty–five (25) minutes.
4. Serve with mashed cooked Irish potatoes or steamed brown rice.

KALE with GARLIC and SESAME SEEDS

INGREDIENTS:
- 1 bunch fresh kale
- 1 tsp olive or coconut oil
- 1 tsp minced garlic
- 2 Tbsps. sesame seeds
- ¼ tsp sea salt
- 2 Tbsps. water

DIRECTIONS:
1. Wash kale by rinsing or submerging in bowl of water and swishing it around. Pull leafy parts from stems. Discard stems. Tear leaves into bite-sized pieces.
2. Heat large skillet or wok over high heat for a minute. Then add 2 tablespoons of water.
3. Add garlic and cook for about 15–20 seconds until it starts to smell fragrant. Add sesame seeds and half the kale. Sprinkle with half the salt and toss around a few minutes until kale starts to wilt. Add remaining kale and continue to cook until it's softened and reduced in volume by half. It should still be bright green.
4. Remove from heat and sprinkle with coconut oil. Serve hot or at room temperature.

TOASTED COUSCOUS with GARLIC and SCALLION

Toasting gives couscous more flavor. Warm 1 tablespoon of coconut oil in a saucepan. Stir in 1 cup couscous until it smells fragrant and toasty. Boil water separately, pour over couscous, and proceed as normal or do untoasted version below.

INGREDIENTS:
- 1 cup instant couscous
- 1 Tbsps. coconut oil
- 1 cup water or broth
- ½ tsp sea salt
- ¼ tsp garlic powder
- ½ tsp turmeric powder

- 1 stalk scallion finely chopped

DIRECTIONS:
1. **Bring water to a boil:** Pour water and oil (if using) into a small saucepan and bring it to a boil over high heat.
2. **Stir in couscous:** Remove pan from heat and pour in couscous, scallion, garlic powder, turmeric and salt. Stir to evenly moisten couscous.
3. **Wait 10 minutes:** Cover pan and let it sit for 10 minutes. If couscous hasn't absorbed the water or still tastes crunchy after this time, cover and let it sit for a few more minutes.
4. **Fluff with a fork:** Gently break apart and fluff cooked couscous with a fork before serving. If the rest of dinner isn't quite done, re-cover pan after fluffing to keep couscous warm. Enjoy with bean or peas stew and a lovely raw vegetable salad.

STEAMED SPANISH NEEDLE and CALLALOO

INGREDIENTS:
- 2 tsps. coconut oil
- ¼ tsp sea salt
- 1 small purple or white onion julienne
- Dash of cayenne pepper (*optional*)
- 2 cups chopped Callaloo
- 1 cup chopped Spanish Needle leaves
- 1-ounce scallion chopped
- 2 garlic cloves diced

DIRECTIONS:
1. In a sauté pot over medium flame, add oil and sauté onions, garlic and scallion for 1 minute (*you don't have to use oil, it can also be done in just water*).
2. Add chopped callaloo, Spanish needle leaves and salt, cover and continue cooking for another 5 minutes, until the callaloo and Spanish needle are tender.
NOTE: *The tender plant parts of the Spanish Needle are excellent for the bowels. The most tender leaves and stem of a plant that has not yet begun to flower, is the ones we choose for steaming and eating as a vegetable. It is anti-inflammatory, antimicrobial, nutritive, vermifuge (destroys or expels parasite and worms), vulnerary (for the healing of wounds)*

CREAMY COCONUT KALE with ONIONS

INGREDIENTS:
- 1 bunch fresh kale
- ¼ cup coconut milk
- ½ small purple onion sliced
- 1 tsp wheat germ oil
- 1 tsp minced garlic
- 2 Tbsps. sesame seeds
- ¼ tsp sea salt

DIRECTIONS:
1. Wash kale by rinsing or submerging in a bowl of water and swishing it around. Pull leafy parts from stems. Discard stems. Tear leaves into bite-sized pieces.
2. Heat large skillet or wok over high heat for a minute. Then add coconut milk.
3. Add garlic and onion, cook only about 1 minute until it starts to smell fragrant. Add sesame seeds and kale.
4. Sprinkle with salt and toss around a few minutes (*about 3 minutes*) until kale starts to wilt. It should still be bright green. Remove from heat and sprinkle with wheat germ oil. Serve hot or at room temperature.

STEAMED ACKEE

INGREDIENTS:
- 2 cups ackee cleaned and washed
- ½ tsp sea salt
- ½ tsp turmeric powder
- ¼ cup red or yellow bell pepper diced
- 2 small tomatoes diced
- 2 scallion stalks diced
- 1 small purple onion diced
- 1 sprig fresh thyme
- 2 garlic cloves diced
- 4 Tbsps. cold pressed (virgin) coconut oil
- Herbal seasons: basil, sage, oregano (*dash to taste*)
- ⅛ cup pure water

DIRECTIONS:
1. Put the stove on low to medium heat, and in a stainless steel pot add oil, bell pepper, scallion, onion, thyme, tomatoes and garlic. Cook for 1–2 minutes until tender.
2. Add uncooked ackee, salt, turmeric, herbs and water. Reduce stove to very low heat and let steam for 15–20 minutes. Enjoy with roasted breadfruit, boiled bananas, steamed string beans, and steamed pumpkin, home-made flaxseed or pumpkin bread.

STEAMED QUINOA with PUMPKIN

INGREDIENTS:
- 1 cup uncooked quinoa (*white or golden, red, or black*)
- Olive oil (*optional*)
- 2 cups water or broth
- ½ tsp sea salt
- ½ cup grated pumpkin

DIRECTIONS:
1. **Rinse quinoa:** Place quinoa into a fine-mesh strainer. Rinse thoroughly with cool water for about 2 minutes. Rub and swish quinoa with your hand while rinsing. Drain.
2. **Toast quinoa in saucepan (optional):** Heat a drizzle of olive oil in saucepan over medium-high heat, and add drained quinoa. Cook, stirring, for about 1 minute to let water evaporate and toast quinoa.
3. **Add liquid and bring to a boil:** Stir in water or broth, grated pumpkin and salt. Bring to a rolling boil.
4. **Lower heat and cook, covered, for 15 minutes.** Turn heat down to lowest setting. Cover and cook for 15 minutes. **Let stand, covered, for 5 minutes:** Remove pot from heat and let stand for 5 more minutes, covered.
5. **Fluff and eat.** Remove lid (*You should see tiny spirals (the germ) separating from and curling around quinoa seeds*).
6. Fluff quinoa gently with a fork, and serve. *If any liquid remains in bottom of pan or if quinoa is still a bit crunchy, return pot to low heat and cook, covered, for another 5 minutes, until all the water has been absorbed.*

STEAMED CABBAGE and CARROT CURRY

INGREDIENTS:
- 1 cabbage chopped
- 2 carrots grated
- ½ cup bell pepper chopped
- 1 onion chopped
- 1 garlic clove minced
- 2 Tbsps. coconut oil
- ⅛ tsp coriander powder
- 1 tsp sea salt
- ¼ cup water
- 1 tsp turmeric powder

DIRECTIONS:
1. Sauté onion, garlic and peppers in two tablespoons of water then add carrot and cabbage.
2. Stir for a minute then add in turmeric, coriander and sea salt. Add water as needed.
3. Cover and steam for a minute or two until tender but still crunchy.
4. Add coconut oil after the stove has been turned off to enhance the flavor.

CURRIED BREADFRUIT DELIGHT

INGREDIENTS:
- 1 cup pure water
- 2 Tbsps. coconut oil
- 1 tsp turmeric powder
- ½ green mature *(fit)* breadfruit
- 1 scallion stalk
- 1 small onion diced
- ½ red or yellow bell pepper diced
- 2 sprigs fresh thyme
- 1 garlic clove
- ½ tsp sea salt
- Herbs: basil, sage, parsley, oregano

DIRECTIONS:
1. Wash breadfruit. Remove skin, cut into chunk size pieces (about 1 inch thick).
2. Chop seasonings in preparation to sauté. With ½ cup of water mix the turmeric powder.
3. Heat oil and sauté seasonings (onions, bell pepper, onion, scallion, thyme, garlic) with the dried herbs, stirring continuously. Steam seasonings in water and add coconut oil after you have completed the dish.
4. Add breadfruit to the pot and the turmeric water. Add salt to taste. Cover and simmer until tender.
5. Serve with favorite bean or peas stew, string beans and a tomato and cucumber salad.

OKRA and GINGER COOKED JAMAICAN STYLEY

This dish is easy to make and healthy for you. It goes well with a simple bean stew, brown rice or steamed pumpkin and yam.

INGREDIENTS:
- 1 lb. okra washed and patted dry with a cloth. Okra must be dry before it is cut.
- 2 Tbsps. coconut oil
- 1 tsp. ginger minced
- 1 medium onion sliced fine lengthwise
- 1 tsp. sea salt
- 1 tsp. whole cumin
- ½ tsp. turmeric powder
- ½ tsp. garlic powder

DIRECTIONS:
1. Cut okra in thin slices. Heat coconut oil on medium heat in a stainless steel skillet or iron skillet.
2. Add cumin and onions and fry until light brown. Add okra and ginger.
3. Fry uncovered until the okra cooks and turns brown. Add turmeric, garlic powder and sea salt.

TIP: If you don't want to fry your okra, you can combine all the ingredients in a bowl, then pour out on a baking sheet and bake at 350°F for 20 minutes.

SWEET and SOUR CAULIFLOWER BALLS

INGREDIENTS:
- 1 head cauliflower
- 6 Tbsps. chick pea or soy flour
- 2 Tbsps. arrowroot powder
- 1 tsp. garlic powder
- 1 tsp. ginger powder or minced ginger
- 1 tsp. sea salt
- 6 Tbsps. pure water
- 1 Tbsp. coconut oil
- 2 Tbsps. onion or scallion chopped

Sauce:
- 1 ¼ tsps. olive oil
- ½ cup onion chopped
- 3 garlic cloves minced
- 2 tsps. ginger grated
- 2 Tbsps. bell pepper finely diced
- 1 tsp. ground coriander
- ¼ tsp. turmeric powder
- 1 tsp. lemon juice
- 1 Tbsp. agave or maple syrup
- 2 tsps. arrowroot powder
- ¼ cup water

DIRECTIONS:

For Sauce:
1. In a sauté pan over medium heat, warm oil.
2. Add onion and sauté for 2 minutes.
3. Add garlic, ginger and bell pepper and sauté for another minute. Add coriander and turmeric and stir fry for 1 minute. Add lemon juice and agave or maple syrup. Bring to a simmer.
4. In a small bowl, stir together arrowroot powder and water. Whisk arrowroot powder into sauce and simmer for a few minutes. Keep warm.

For Cauliflower Balls:

1. Preheat oven to 350°F with a baking sheet in the oven. (*Baking sheet should not be non-stick*).
2. Cut cauliflower into 1 inch florets. In a large bowl, whisk together flour, arrowroot powder, garlic powder, ginger powder and salt. Whisk in seltzer water. Pour oil on hot baking sheet and spread around to fully cover baking sheet. Quickly dip florets into the batter and place on baking sheet.
3. Bake for 10 minutes. Flip cauliflower and bake for another 10 minutes. Pour sauce over cauliflower and toss to cover cauliflower completely in sauce. Sprinkle with diced scallion (chives) and serve immediately.

CABBAGE CASHEW STIR FRY

INGREDIENTS:
- Handful cashew nuts
- 4 tsps. olive or cold pressed coconut oil
- 1 onion peeled and diced
- ½ red or yellow bell pepper stemmed and roughly chopped
- 2" fresh ginger peeled and roughly chopped
- 4 garlic cloves diced
- Half head cabbage (small or medium, halved and sliced)
- 1 tsp. turmeric powder
- 6 Tbsps. spring or filtered water
- ¼ – ½ tsp Sea salt to taste
- 1 tsp. chives chopped
- 1 tsp. fresh parsley leaves chopped

DIRECTIONS:
1. Heat olive oil in a large skillet over high heat. Stir in onion, garlic, yellow bell pepper, minced ginger, scallion and turmeric. Stirring every 30 seconds. Add washed and chopped cabbage and stir.
2. Add herbs (chives and parsley leaves) and let steam until tender for approximately 3 minutes.
3. Add salt and then chopped cashew nuts. Turn off the stove and let heat finish bringing all the flavors together.

QUINOA and VEGETABLE STIR FRY

INGREDIENTS:
- ½ cup Quinoa (soaked overnight in fresh spring water)
- ¼ cup purple onion finely chopped
- 1 scallion stalk
- 2 garlic cloves roasted minced or finely chopped
- 1–2 thumb–size ginger sliced into thin matchstick pieces
- ¼ cup red or yellow bell pepper chopped
- ¼ cup carrots coarsely shredded
- 2 cups washed snow peas
- 1 cup spinach chopped
- ½ small head cauliflower cut into bit sized pieces
- ¼ tsp basil, parsley and dill (*dried or fresh herbs*)
- 2 Tbsps. coconut or olive oil
- Pinch sea salt
- Few pieces of cashew (optional)

DIRECTIONS:
1. Warm a wok or large frying pan over medium–high heat. Add oil and swirl around, then add onion, scallion, bell pepper, garlic and ginger. Stir fry 1–2 minutes.
2. Add cauliflower, carrots, snow peas and spinach. Stir fry 2 minutes and add the salt.
3. Drain and rinse the Quinoa which has been soaking overnight.
4. Add the Quinoa to the vegetables and stir for another minute.
5. Remove from heat and top with fresh parsley and cashew or almond nuts (optional).
6. Serve over steamed brown rice or with steamed yam, pumpkin, and sweet potatoes.

MIXED VEGETABLE STIR FRY with CASHEW NUTS

INGREDIENTS:
- 1 Tbsp. coconut oil
- 1 medium bell pepper diced
- 1 cup cauliflower florets
- 1 cup broccoli florets
- 1 cup sugar snap peas sliced
- 2 cups callaloo or spinach chopped
- 1 cup raw cashew nuts
- 2 garlic cloves diced
- 1 medium onion diced
- 3 scallion stalks diced
- ½ tsp garlic powder
- 1 tsp maple syrup or honey (optional)
- ½ tsp sea salt
- Small piece ginger grated or ginger powder

DIRECTIONS:
1. Heat two tablespoons of water in wok or large deep skillet on medium–high heat.
2. Add onion, scallion, bell pepper and garlic. Stir fry for 2 minutes.
3. Add remaining vegetables. Stir fry for 5 to 7 minutes or until vegetables are tender–crisp.
4. Add salt, honey, garlic powder and ginger. Stir fry until well blended. Serve over cooked brown rice, if desired.
5. Add the coconut oil last just before serving.

JACKFRUIT BBQ STIR FRY

INGREDIENTS:
- 2 sweet peppers finely chopped
- 2 Tbsps. coconut oil
- 6 cloves garlic finely chopped
- 1 medium onion chopped
- 2 tsps. cumin powder
- ½ tsp. cayenne
- ½ cup tomato paste or tomatoes diced
- ¼ cup lime or lemon juice (*more if you like it tangy*)
- 1 cup raw honey
- 1 tsp. turmeric powder
- 5 Tbsps. molasses
- 4 cups of ripe jackfruit pegged
- ½ tsp. coriander powder

DIRECTIONS:
1. Fry the garlic, onions, scallion and bell pepper in oil for one minute.
2. Add all the spices, stir and cook until fragrant for a minute or so.
3. Add tomato paste, lime and honey. Stir until all combined.
4. Partially cover and keep cooking on low heat until sauce has thickened to the consistency of ketchup.
5. Put the pegged jackfruit into a bowl.
6. Heat oil in pan and add the pegged jackfruit. Cook until it gets a bit grey and loses some moisture.
7. Add the turmeric powder and stir in. Add a little water if it starts to stick to the pan.
8. Add about half the BBQ sauce (*more if you want a very sticky dish*) and stir in to coat.
9. Cook until it begins to get a little crispy and sticking to the pan.
10. Serve with steamed or raw pumpkin and string beans, or a tomato, cucumber, purple onion and bell pepper salad. Goes well also with roasted breadfruit or steamed yam and boiled green bananas.

KALE, PAK CHOY and CARROT STIR FRY

INGREDIENTS:
- 1 small purple or yellow onion
- 2 cloves garlic
- 2 Tbsps. olive or coconut oil
- 1 medium carrot shredded
- 1 Tbsp. dried parsley heaping
- ¼ cup coconut milk, water or vegetable stock
- 3 stalks scallion
- 2 bunch Pak Choy chopped
- 2 cups kale de-stemmed, finely chopped
- ½ tsp. sea salt to taste
- ¼ tsp. grated ginger

DIRECTIONS:
1. Sauté onion, scallion and garlic in coconut oil for about 1 minute. Stirring.
2. Add coconut milk, water or vegetable stock. Add ginger, shredded carrots, parsley, kale and Pak Choy.
3. Cook 2 minutes. Stirring. Simmer until vegetables are softened. Add salt to taste.
4. Simmer another 2–3 minutes until vegetables are thoroughly cooked.

ROASTED ONIONS with RED-SKINNED POTATOES and SWEET POTATOES

INGREDIENTS:
- 2 cups (sweet) purple onions cut into slivers (*2 large onions*)
- 1 cup small red-skinned potatoes
- 1 cup sweet potatoes washed, peeled and diced
- 1 red bell pepper
- ½ tsp sea salt to taste
- 1 tsp paprika
- ½ tsp rosemary
- 2 Tbsps. virgin olive oil

DIRECTIONS:
1. Preheat oven to 400°F.
2. Spray a large rectangular baking dish with non-stick spray or line out baking sheet with parchment paper.
3. Add slivered onions to baking dish. Thoroughly wash red-skinned potatoes (*do not peel*) and cut into fourths.
4. Add peeled and diced sweet potatoes. Add to onions.
5. Wash bell pepper. Remove stem end and seeds. Slice into thin slivers and add to potatoes and onions.
6. Sprinkle salt, paprika and rosemary over vegetables. Drizzle olive oil over all and toss with your fingers or a couple of forks until all is evenly coated with the oil. Place in preheated oven and bake for at least one (1) hour. Some of the onions and potato wedges will begin to brown. Remove and serve hot.

Dumplings, Rice, Bulgur, Millet, Almond Nut & Meat

15 Recipes

VEGGIE CURRY with LENTIL SPELT FLOUR DUMPLINGS

INGREDIENTS:
- 2 small Irish potatoes
- 2 small carrots
- 1 cup shredded callaloo
- 1 cup shredded cabbage
- ½ cup coconut milk
- 2 Tbsps. olive or virgin coconut oil
- ¼ tsp. sea salt
- 1 tsp turmeric powder
- 1 medium onion
- 2 scallion stalks
- Dash cumin, coriander, garlic powder, paprika, cayenne pepper, parsley, ginger

DIRECTIONS:
1. In a pot over medium heat, sauté onion and scallion in a bit of water or coconut oil.
2. Add coconut milk, diced potato and carrots. Add in herbs and salt. Let simmer for 10–15 minutes on low heat. Add cabbage and callaloo. Stir and let simmer for 2 minutes.
3. Turn off stove and enjoy with your Lentil Spelt Flour dumplings.
   (**Optional**: add coconut oil at the end of the cooking process to preserve the nutritional properties of the oil).

LENTIL SPELT FLOUR DUMPLINGS

INGREDIENTS:
- 1 cup spelt flour
- ½ cup lentils (*soaked overnight or for three hours – makes cooking time shorter*)
- 1/8 tsp. sea salt
- 3 Tbsps. wheat germ
- ¼ cup or less water to combine and make dough
- 1 medium pot filled with water to boil dumplings

DIRECTIONS:
1. Combine all ingredients in a bowl. Add water slowly as you use a spoon to combine.
2. Remove the spoon once you have loose dough.
3. Knead dough using your hands, adding flour, until it no longer sticks to your fingers.
4. Break into small pieces and make your dumplings. Add to a pot of boiling water and cook for 45 minutes.

SPELT FLOUR OATS DUMPLINGS

INGREDIENTS:
- 2 cups spelt flour
- ½ tsp. sea salt
- ¼ cup rolled oats flour
- ½ cup cold water

DIRECTIONS:
1. Pour the spelt flour, oats flour, and salt together into a large mixing bowl.
2. Add the water 3 teaspoons at a time, just enough to bring the dough together with a firm consistency.
3. On a lightly floured surface, knead the dough well, for about five minutes. Bring a pot of water to boil.
4. Break off pieces and form the dough into slightly flattened biscuits, about 2 inches across.
5. For spinners roll the pieces between your palms into a pen shape. Place the pieces into the pot of hot water.
6. Let cook for approximately 1 hour at low heat.

BAKED COCONUT CHICKPEAS DUMPLINGS

INGREDIENTS:
- 2 cups spelt flour
- 1 cup chickpea flour
- 1 tsp. sea salt
- ¼ cup olive oil
- ½ cup unsweetened dried coconut
- 1 cup water
- ¼ tsp. garlic powder

DIRECTIONS:
1. Preheat oven to 300°F.
2. Place all ingredients into mixing bowl and combine to make a dough.
3. Divide into ten to twelve small round dough pieces, place on baking sheet and bake for 30–40 minutes.
4. Remove from oven and serve with peas or bean stew, steamed or raw vegetable salad.

DEBRA'S SWEET POTATO CASSEROLE

INGREDIENTS:
- 4 cups (*about 2–3 pounds*) sweet potatoes boiled or steamed peeled and cubed
- ¼ cup virgin coconut oil
- ¼ cup raw honey
- 1 tsp coriander powder
- ¼ cup rice, almond or coconut milk
- 2 Tbsps. flaxseed powder
- 1 tsp grated ginger
- ½ tsp sage
- ½ tsp salt

Topping:
- 2 cups wholegrain flakes, crushed – *purchase from a health food store (for 1 ½ cups crumbs)*
- ¼ cup pecans or walnuts finely chopped

DIRECTIONS:
1. Preheat oven to 350°F.
2. Spray a shallow 2-quart casserole dish with cooking oil spray and set aside.
3. In a large bowl of an electric mixer (*or a hand mixer*) blend well all casserole ingredients until well-mixed.
4. Spread into prepared casserole dish. In medium bowl, mix together topping ingredients and sprinkle over top of sweet potato mixture.
5. Bake for 30 minutes or until golden on edges and topping is crispy.
6. (*At 30 minutes, check to make sure topping is not too brown. Some ovens prove too hot for the delicate topping. If topping begins to get too dark, cover with foil and continue to bake for remaining 15 minutes, uncovering only in the last few minutes of baking to insure a crisp topping*).

CARROT BALLS with SWEET and SOUR SAUCE

INGREDIENTS:
- 2 large carrots
- 1 cup toasted oatmeal flour
- 1 medium onion chopped very thin
- ½ tsp sea salt
- ½ tsp thyme
- 3 cloves garlic chopped
- 4 Tbsps. flax seed gel (*to replace eggs*)
- ¼ cup coconut oil
- ¼ cup red sweet pepper diced very thin
- ¼ cup yellow sweet pepper diced
- 1 stalk celery sliced
- 3 stalks scallion chopped
- ¼ cup tomato diced
- 2 Tbsps. lemon juice
- ½ cup water
- 1 ½ Tbsps. mixed herbs (*basil, sage, parsley, coriander*)
- 2 tsps. honey
- 1 tsp molasses
- 1 tsp grated ginger

Carrot Balls served with Debra's Sweet Potato Casserole and steamed cauliflower and broccoli!

DIRECTIONS:
1. Shred carrots and place in a large mixing bowl.
2. Add oats flour or breadcrumbs, onion, scallion, salt, thyme, herbs and garlic.
3. Whisk flax seed gel and add to mixture. Use hand to bind mixture and make balls. Cover and leave to marinate for about 10 minutes.
4. Bake in oven for 30 minutes at 350°F, or fry them (*I don't recommend too many fried foods in the diet*). To fry: heat coconut oil in frying pan. Shape carrot balls using 2 Tbsps. of mixture for each and fry until they are brown on all sides. Drain on absorbent paper.

TO MAKE SWEET AND SOUR SAUCE:

1. Put one tablespoon of oil in a frying pan. Heat and use to sauté sweet peppers, celery and onions.
2. Blend tomato in water and pour into pan. Mix in lemon juice, honey, molasses, coriander, sage, ginger, celery basil and salt. Allow to simmer for about ten minutes.
3. Add carrot balls and simmer for 5 minutes or drizzle over carrot balls when you are about to eat them.

COCONUT CURRIED LENTILS and BROWN RICE

INGREDIENTS:
- 2 Tbsps. virgin coconut oil
- 1 Tbsp. turmeric powder
- ¼ tsp sage, coriander, cumin (mixed)
- ¼ cup onion thinly sliced
- 1 Tbsp. ginger finely minced
- 3 garlic cloves chopped
- 3 scallion stalks diced
- 1 sprig thyme
- 1 cup brown rice (soaked overnight)
- 1 cup pure water
- 1 cup lentils
- ½ tsp cumin seed
- 1 cup coconut milk
- ½ tsp sea salt
- 1 cup cilantro chopped

DIRECTIONS:
1. Heat the oil, turmeric, sage, cumin, garlic and coriander together in a large Dutch oven or soup pot set over medium heat. Add the onion, scallion and thyme and cook, stirring occasionally for 2–3 minutes, or until deeply golden and very soft. Add the ginger and cook, stirring, until softened, 1 more minute.
2. Add the rice, water, lentils and cumin seed and bring to a boil. Cover, reduce heat and cook until lentils and rice are tender, about 15 minutes.
3. Stir in the coconut milk and sea salt. Cook for another 20 minutes until rice is done. Garnish with cilantro just before serving.

PINTO BEAN BROWN RICE

INGREDIENTS:
- 4 cups cooked brown rice
- 1 Tbsp. coconut oil
- 1 yellow onion diced
- 1 red bell pepper diced
- 3 stalks scallion diced
- 2 garlic cloves finely diced
- 1 tsp sage
- 1 tsp turmeric
- 1 tsp sea salt
- 1 cup diced tomatoes
- 2 cups cooked pinto beans
- ½ cup shredded carrot

DIRECTIONS:
1. Heat the oil in a large stainless steel skillet. Sauté the onion and bell peppers until the onion is translucent, about 5 minutes. Add the garlic and scallion, and then cook 5 more minutes.
2. Add diced tomatoes, carrots, turmeric, salt and sage. Add beans and rice to heat through. Serve.

SEASONED VEGETABLE RICE

INGREDIENTS:
- 2 Tbsps. cold pressed coconut or olive oil
- 1 ½ cups long-grain brown rice
- ½ cup chopped onion
- ½ cup chopped green bell pepper
- 1 clove garlic minced
- 2 cups water or coconut milk for a richer taste
- 1 tsp sea salt
- ½ cup diced tomatoes
- ½ cup shredded pumpkin
- ½ tsp sea salt to taste
- ½ cup cooked green peas

- ½ cup string beans diced

DIRECTIONS:
1. Soak brown rice overnight in 2 cups of water, this makes it easier to cook and allows a shorter cooking time. In large saucepan, pour out cold pressed oil over medium heat. Add rice, onion, peppers, and garlic.
2. Cook until the rice is toasted. Stir in the water, tomatoes and salt and bring to a boil.
3. Reduce heat and simmer, cover, until the rice is tender, about 20 to 25 minutes.
4. Stir in the pumpkin, green peas, string beans and let steam for another 10 minutes.
5. Transfer to a serving bowl and serve with your favorite bean or pea stew.

ACKEE SEASONED RICE

INGREDIENTS:
- 2 cups ackees picked and washed
- 2 small tomatoes diced
- 2 scallion stalk chopped
- ¼ onion diced
- 1 sprig thyme
- ½ tsp sea salt
- 3 garlic gloves diced
- 2 cups brown rice
- 3 cups pure water
- Dash cayenne pepper to taste
- 2 Tbsps. coconut oil
- 1 Tbsps. turmeric
- ¼ cup red or yellow sweet pepper diced

DIRECTIONS:
1. Put brown rice to soak overnight so it cooks faster. In cooking pot, pour in coconut oil, garlic, scallion, onion, thyme and tomatoes. Stir for about 1 minute until tender.
2. Pour in water, washed and soaked brown rice, salt, sweet pepper, turmeric and ackees. Bring to a boil.
3. Reduce heat and steam for approximately 30 minutes. Serve with baked ripe plantain, avocado and a lovely salad.
4. For more protein serve this with bean or peas stew.

ACKEE LENTIL SEASONED RICE

INGREDIENTS:
- 1 cup lentils (*boil for 10 minutes, wash and throw off water*)
- 1 cup brown rice
- 2 cups ackees picked and cleaned (*can use more or less*)
- 1 cup pumpkin diced
- 1 large onion diced
- 3 stalks scallion chopped
- ¼ medium red or yellow bell pepper diced
- 4 cloves garlic
- 1 tsp turmeric powder
- ½ tsp sea salt
- Herbs: sage, cumin, basil, parsley, oregano
- 4 cups water (*or 2 cups water and 2 cups coconut milk*)

DIRECTIONS:
1. In a stainless steel pot, pour four teaspoons water, add onions, garlic, scallion and bell pepper.
2. Stir for 2 minutes, and then add salt, 4 cups water, herbs, rice, lentils, pumpkin and ackees.
3. Bring to a boil, then turn stove down to low heat and let simmer for 30 minutes or until rice is cooked light and fluffy. Serve with raw salad and a few avocado slices.

CARROT WALNUT ALMOND MEAT

INGREDIENTS:
- 1 cup raw almonds soaked
- ½ cup walnuts
- 2 cups shredded carrots
- 2 clove garlic
- 1 small onion
- 2 scallion stalks
- 2 Tbsps. cold pressed coconut or olive oil
- 1 tsp dried basil leaves
- ⅛ tsp. cayenne pepper
- ½ tsp. sea salt
- 4 tsps. red sweet pepper chopped
- Dash onion and garlic powder
- ½ tsp. thyme leaf

DIRECTIONS:
1. In food processor, grind almonds, walnuts and carrots until no large chunks are visible.
2. Pulse in garlic, onion, scallion, salt, sweet pepper and additional herbs.
3. Eat Carrot-Walnut-Almond meat right away, or let sit in fridge for a while to let the flavor develop. Nut meat should be kept in the refrigerator for around four or five days.
4. Enjoy in lettuce wraps, carrot sticks, raw pumpkin slices, celery sticks, cucumber or have with anything you would normally have meat with. This is healthy, protein packed and delicious!

ALMOND NUT MEAT

INGREDIENTS:
- 2 cups raw almonds soaked
- ½ cup sunflower seeds and/or pumpkin seeds (*optional*)
- 1 clove garlic
- 1 onion
- 2 scallion stalks
- 2 Tbsps. cold pressed coconut or olive oil
- 1 tsp dried basil leaves
- 3 Tbsps. turmeric
- 1 tsp. sea salt
- ½ Tbsp. mixed spices
- 1 tsp. chopped sweet pepper
- Dash onion powder & garlic powder
- ½ tsp. thyme leaf

For Mexican style nut meat:
- Cumin, chili powder, cayenne, coriander, paprika, cilantro, lime.

For Italian style nut meat:
- Sage, thyme, rosemary, oregano, basil, marjoram, sun dried tomatoes.

DIRECTIONS:
1. In your food processor, grind almonds, sunflower and or or pumpkin seeds until no large chunks are visible.
2. Pulse in the garlic, onion, scallion, salt, pepper and additional spices.
3. Add walnuts and blend until a coarse crumb like consistency is reached.
4. You can eat your nut meat right away, or let it sit in the refrigerator for a while to let the flavor develop. Nut meat should be kept in the refrigerator for around four or five days.
5. Enjoy in lettuce wraps or with carrot sticks, celery sticks, or anywhere you would usually use meat.

ALMOND NUT MEAT served with FRESH VEGETABLE SALAD

Wrap the Almond Nut meat in Cabbage Leaves for a "Raw Taco".

Put the Almond Nut meat in Romaine Lettuce Boats.

Mango (or pineapple), sweet pepper and corn combined with the almond nut meat.

CHICKPEA FLOUR TOFU

INGREDIENTS:
- 1 cup chickpea or garbanzo bean flour
- ½ to ¾ tsp. Celtic or Himalayan sea salt
- ¼ tsp. garlic powder
- ½ tsp. turmeric
- ¼ tsp. cumin
- 1¾ cups water
- Herbs to your liking: basil, sage, dill, chives, parsley

DIRECTIONS:
1. Grease bread dish or line with parchment and keep ready. (*9 x 5 rectangle or any similar rectangle or smaller square pan*).
2. In a bowl place all dry ingredients, then add water slowly, whisk all ingredients until there are no lumps (*or use a blender*).
3. Pour chickpea flour mixture into a deep saucepan with ½ cup of boiling water. Cook over low heat. Stir continuously. Mixture will begin to have a porridge consistency. Keep stirring for about 2–3 minutes.

4. Once mixture is evenly thick and stiff, keep cooking for another 1–2 minutes so chickpea flour gets cooked through. Tap spoon or spatula to drop mixture stuck to it to the pan. You can taste test the mixture at this point carefully, to ensure that there is no raw chickpea flour flavor and adjust more salt if needed.
5. Pour mixture into prepared loaf dish and even it out using a spatula if needed. Let it cool, then refrigerate for at least an hour to set.
6. Remove the set slab from pan. Slice into cubes. Store in an airtight container for up to 4 days. The tofu can leak some moisture while it sits. Drain and use.

Use chickpea tofu to make vegetable stir fry dishes, a sweet and sour dish by adding honey and lemon juice, make a gravy using blended sunflower seeds, herbs and spices and simmer down with the tofu. Enjoy with your grains like brown rice, quinoa, millet etc., vegetables like sprouts, cabbage, carrots, callaloo, spinach etc., savory fruits like tomatoes, cucumbers, okra, pumpkin, zucchini etc.

BETTER TO HAVE YOUR VEGETABLES STEAMED

Steaming vegetables breaks down the plants' cell walls, releasing more of the nutrients bound to those cell walls. Steamed vegetables supply more antioxidants, including beta-carotene, lutein and lycopene, than they do when raw. When you eat your veggies — which, you know, you should be doing two to three times a day, you may be of the belief that, in order to gain all the benefits they have to offer, you must eat them raw, but this is not so.

Many people eat raw kale without any issues (most major chopped salad chains wouldn't exist otherwise) but it can have negative effects on others. Lettuce is one of the few greens that can be eaten raw with no negative side effect on the stomach. That said, context is key here, you would probably have to eat an excessive amount of raw kale for it to negatively impact the thyroid, so, unless you're eating a bushel of raw kale a day, you're probably in the clear.

Tomatoes certainly have many health benefits when eaten raw. But if you eat a lot of raw tomatoes, it might be worth giving them some heat every now and then, if only for the sake of variety. According to a study published in the Journal of Agricultural and Food Chemistry, tomatoes release more lycopene (a cancer-fighting antioxidant) when cooked. According to Scientific American, this is because the heat can break down some tougher cell walls in the plant, making it easier for the body to absorb their nutrients.

According to Scientific American, cooking cruciferous vegetables such as broccoli, cauliflower, and cabbage helps them release indole, an organic compound that can fight off precancerous cells. Raw cruciferous vegetables have also been known to cause digestive problems for some people. "You can eat these veggies raw, but to curtail the digestive issues that may arise, try them in small quantities, chew them well, and if your system is not used to them, don't eat them all together at one sitting. You'll have an easier time moving them through your system if they are cooked vs. eating them raw. Steaming carrots can help them release carotenoids, an antioxidant that helps with overall immune function

Peppers are another great source of lycopene and ferulic acid — and, obviously, you'll benefit from those nutrients however you choose to eat them. But roasting or stir-frying bell peppers every now and then can help you absorb more of their vitamins, as long as you don't overdo the heat.

Source - https://www.insider.com/vegetables-better-cooked-than-raw-2...

AN OPTIMUM HEALTH COOK'S GUIDE

_____Some Important Points to Consider_____

Salt
Salt is essential to making good blood.
The best salt to use would be one that has iodine and other trace minerals. Iodine is essential in regulating the thyroid function. Without it, one may develop thyroid related conditions, including goiter and greaves disease. You can purchase Celtic (light gray in colour) or Himalayan (pink in colour) sea salt at any health food store

Sodium Bicarbonate
The use of soda or baking powder in bread making is harmful and unnecessary. Soda causes inflammation of the stomach, and often poisons the entire system. (CD p. 342)

Sodium bicarbonate found in baking powder and baking soda irritates the stomach and causes the PH level in the stomach to remain high, thus preventing the manufacture of the intrinsic factor which is essential in breaking down protein in the stomach and the production of vitamin B12 in the intestines. High PH levels 2 prevent the digestion of protein in the stomach. It would be wise therefore, to avoid the use of items containing sodium bicarbonate.

Sugar
Sugar is not good for the stomach. It causes fermentation and this clouds the brain and brings peevishness into the disposition. (CD p. 327)
It clogs the system …affects the brain directly and …sugar when largely used, is more injurious than meat (CD p. 328)

Use natural sugars: Honey, Agave nectar, Molasses, Dates, Organic raisins, Bananas, Apple sauce, Cane juice.
Concentrated sugars, even good sweeteners like honey and agave nectar should be used sparingly.
"I frequently sit down to the tables of the brethren and sisters, and see that they use a great amount of milk and sugar. These clog the system, irritate the digestive organs, and affect the brain. Anything that hinders the active motion of the living machinery affects the brain very directly. And from the light given me, sugar, when largely used, is more injurious than meat." – Counsels on Health pg. 150, Ellen G. White

Sugar consumption linked to breast cancer and its spread to other organs, scientists say - CARIBBEAN360 Magazine - JANUARY 5, 2016: A common sugar found in fizzy drinks like colas and food such as cereal bars, biscuits and ketchup could be driving breast cancer, a new study suggests. The high-sugar Western diet may not only increase the risk of breast cancer, but the potential for it to spread to the lungs, scientists warn.

Condiments, Spices, Fermented Items

Avoid all condiments, mustards, mayonnaise, vegennaise, nayonnaise, ketchup, vinaigrette dressings, Worcestershire sauce, barbecue sauces.

Avoid all fermented items. These items include but are not limited to:

Vinaigrette dressings, vinegar, apple cider, alcohol, soy sauces, miso, tempeh, tamari, and items of like character. Vinegar depletes calcium phosphate which is an essential mineral element for the formation and strengthening of bones and teeth. Without it our bones can become brittle, pliable and painful thus leading to conditions such as rickets and osteoporosis.

Avoid all spices, ginger, mauby, all energy drinks, curry, nutmeg, mace, cinnamon, cloves in your daily cooking. These items are to be used for medicinal purposes only.

Most spices can be used for medicinal purposes but not for dietary uses (that includes vinegar for external uses).

Avoid all hot peppers (including but not limited to chili peppers, black and white peppers, scotch bonnet, bird pepper, hot pepper sauces, and so forth) are related to cancer of the stomach and hypertension. They are also stimulants and should be avoided. Cayenne pepper can be used for medicinal purposes.

Eating vegetables and fruits at the same meal

Genesis 1:11 defines a fruit as: "... fruit after his kind, whose seed is in itself...". Vegetables do not have seeds within themselves, but fruits do.

It is not well to eat fruit and vegetables at the same meal. If the digestion is feeble, the use of both will often cause distress, and inability to put forth mental effort. It is better to have the fruit at one meal, and the 3 vegetables at another. Fruit and vegetables taken at one meal produce acidity of the stomach; then impurity of the blood results, and the mind is not clear because the digestion is imperfect. (CD p. 112)

Eating unripe or spoiled fruit

Nicely prepared vegetables and fruits in their season will be beneficial, if they are of the best quality, not showing the slightest sign of decay, but are sound and unaffected by any disease or decay. More die by eating decayed fruit and decayed vegetables which ferment in the stomach and result in blood poisoning, than we have any idea of. (CD p. 309)

Eating fruits at the end of a meal

Eat fruits and vegetables at the start of a meal, not the end of the meal as in deserts as some usually do. Eating raw food before the cooked food is eaten prevents the formation of inflammation in the intestines. Watermelon should especially be avoided at the end of a meal. Watermelon as a fruit should not be combined with other fruits, but eaten alone.

Eating bread which was not well baked
If the inside can be squeezed into dough, do not eat it. New raised bread is difficult to digest and is more healthful if eaten two or three days old.

Eating too much liquid food
Too much soups are unhealthful ...so much liquid taken into the stomach was not healthful, and that all who subsisted on such a diet placed a great tax upon the kidneys, and so much watery substance debilitated (*weakened*) the stomach. (CD p. 105)

Eating too great a variety at a meal
Keep it Simple.
Do not have too great a variety at a meal; three or four dishes are a plenty. At the next meal you can have a change. There should not be many kinds at any one meal, but all meals should not be composed of the same kinds of food without variation. (CD p. 110)
The habit of overeating, or of eating too many kinds of food at one meal, frequently causes dyspepsia.

Serious injury is thus done to the delicate digestive organs. In vain the stomach protests, and appeals to the brain to reason from cause to effect. The excessive amount of food eaten, or the improper combination, does its injurious work. In vain do disagreeable premonitions give warning. Suffering is the consequence. Disease takes the place of health. (CD p.111)

Eating fried foods
Foods should be prepared in a simple manner free from grease. Avoid fried food, hydrogenated fat. "Grease cooked in the food renders it difficult of digestion". (CD p. 354)

Frequency of eating meals
It is quite a common custom with the people of the world to eat three times a day, besides eating at irregular intervals between meals; and the last meal is generally the heartiest, and is often taken just before retiring. This is reversing the natural order; a hearty meal should never be taken so late in the day. Should these persons change their practice, and eat but two meals a day, and nothing between meals, not even an apple, a nut, or any kind of fruit, the result would be seen in a good appetite and greatly improved health. --R. and H., 1884, No. 31. p. 84, Para. 2, [Healthful Living by Ellen G. White].

Most people enjoy better health while eating two meals a day than three; others, under their existing circumstances, may require something to eat at supper time; but this meal should be very light. Let no one think himself a criterion for all that everyone must do exactly as he does. --C. T., p. 58. p. 84, Para. 3, [HL].

If the third meal be eaten at all, it should be light, and several hours before going to bed. --H. to L., Chap. 1, p. 55. p. 84, Para. 4, [HL].

The stomach, when we lie down to rest, should have its work all done, that it may enjoy rest, as well as other portions of the body. The work of digestion should not be carried on through any period of the sleeping hours. --H. to L., Chap. 1, p. 56. p. 84, Para. 5, [HL].

If you feel that you must eat at night, take a drink of cold water, and in the morning you will feel much better for not having eaten. --T., V. IV, p. 502. p. 85, Para. 1, [HL].

The stomach may be educated to desire food eight times a day, and feel faint if it is not supplied. But this is no argument in favor of so frequent eating. --R. and H., 1883, No. 19. p. 85, Para. 2, [HL].

OPTIMUM NUTRITION

An Overview

"Eat . . . to the glory of God."

1 Corinthians 10:31

What and when we eat is influenced by many factors:
- Personal preference
- Pleasure
- Ethnic heritage or tradition
- Habit
- Social interactions
- Availability
- Convenience
- Economy
- Positive and negative associations (happy occasions, sickness after eating, used as punishment or reward, etc.)
- Emotional comfort (eating in response to emotions)
- Personal Values (political and environmental views, religious beliefs, etc.)
- Body image (may lead to eating disorders like anorexia or bulimia)
- Health benefit (true or false knowledge)

"It is impossible for those who indulge the appetite to attain to Christian perfection." CD 21

"All are being proved to see whether they will accept the principles of health reform or follow a course of self-indulgence." CD 34

"To keep the body in a healthy condition, in order that all parts of the living machinery may act harmoniously, should be a study of our life." CD 18

History of Nutrition

Nutrition as a science is relatively new. Antoine Lavoisier known as the father of modern chemistry and nutrition, in the late 1700's, recognized that "life is a chemical function". One of his special fields of study was the relationship between oxygen and metabolism.

In 1753, a Scottish Naval surgeon, James Lind, published the first case studies in humans showing the connection between diet and disease. He discovered that men suffering from scurvy with its swollen and bleeding gums, tooth loss, easy bruising and bleeding, and weakness and sometimes death, could be cured by eating citrus fruits (limes). Sailors were soon required to eat citrus on their long voyages and the incidences of scurvy dropped dramatically. British sailors are still called by the nickname "limeys" today. Although the cause of the scurvy was identified by observation and deduction, the treatment was based on trial and error. Not until the early 1900's were vitamins isolated by teams in Poland (Funk), Great Britain (Hopkins), and the United States (McCollum, Goldberger, and Williams), and it was not until the mid-1900s that the healing constituent known as ascorbic acid or vitamin C was isolated.

Nutrition has a significant role in our lives, even before birth. Nutrition is a field of study that constantly changes as we understand more about the function of the cells and the body. Scripture tells us that, "…we are fearfully and wonderfully made…"[i]

Nutritional science is a body of scientific knowledge that measures nutritional requirements of humans for:
1. Growth
2. Maintenance
3. Activity
4. Reproduction

The basic foundation of human nutrition revolves around two fundamental areas of science:
Physical sciences: Biochemistry and physiology
Behavioral sciences: How nutrition affects how we think and who we are.

Nutritional science is a body of scientific knowledge that measures nutritional requirements of humans for: Growth; Maintenance; Activity; and Reproduction

- Nutrition is defined as the study of proper diet that promotes good health.
- Good health requires good food choices.
- Should be based on scientific findings. All true science is compatible with the Word of God.
- Should include a balance and variety of foods selected over a period of time

Summary:
Choices should be primarily based on knowledge of nutrition and principles. "…eat ye that which is good, and let your soul delight itself in fatness." Isaiah 55:2 [ii]

What are nutrients?
Nutrients are substances used in your body for the production of energy and to provide the necessary building blocks for growth, repair and maintenance of its cells, tissues, organs and systems. Nutrients may also protect the body from certain chronic disease.

Nutrients are the basic currency of nutrition: Chemical compounds or elements that produce energy (adenotriphosphate or ATP in the cell), or keep the balance of internal control or homeostasis. The Latin meaning of homeostasis is constant or same state.

Specific chemical compounds are the nutrients in a variety of foods needed by the body. There are about 40 essential nutrients in different combinations, but the six (6) most essential and basic nutrients are listed in their order of importance.

The most vital nutrient that sustains life is: water

Macronutrients (needed in significant quantities) are:
- carbohydrates
- fats
- protein

Micronutrients (needed in small quantities) are:
- vitamins
- minerals

Other constituents of food that we will discuss:
- Phytochemicals
- Fiber

Typical body composition in a 150 lb. healthy person:
- Contains 90 lbs. of water (60%)
- Contains 30 lbs. of fat (20%)
- Contains an additional 30 pounds of compounds containing protein, carbohydrates, and major minerals of the bones (20%)
- With just a fraction of a pound left is made up of vitamins and other minerals.[iii],[iv]
- Chemical analysis of a tomato shows it is primarily water (95%). The 5% solid materials are compounds, mostly carbohydrates, fats, proteins, and fiber. A tiny portion of the solid materials would be vitamins and minerals.

Chemical Composition of Nutrients:
Minerals (the simplest): An element with atoms that are all alike. For example, iron remains iron if the food is raw or cooked, if it is in the red blood cell, when the cell is broken down, and when the iron is lost from the body by excretion. An inorganic nutrient (contains no carbon). Minerals are facilitators of enzyme chemical reactions and are indestructible.

Water (next simplest): Made of two elements—hydrogen and oxygen. An inorganic nutrient (contains no carbon).

Carbohydrate (more complex): An organic compound—contains carbon, an element that is found in all living things. Organic means "alive." The most efficient fuel source (starchy foods convert to glucose).

Fat (more complex): An organic compound. Fats are a source of energy and stored calories, needed for production of hormones and absorption of vitamins A, D, E, and K and are found in cell walls.

Protein (more complex): An organic compound made up of carbon, hydrogen and oxygen (like carbohydrates and fats), but also contain nitrogen which promotes growth and cellular repair, used to form DNA and enzymes.

Vitamins (more complex): Organic compounds needed in small amounts for metabolic processes.

Carbohydrates, fats, proteins, and vitamins all contain carbon, an element found in all living things. Therefore, these four more complex classes of nutrients are called organic compounds which means "alive".

Energy-yielding Nutrients
Three of these organic nutrients are broken down in the body to provide useable energy.
- Carbohydrates
- Fats
- Proteins

Non-energy yielding Nutrients
These nutrients do not yield energy in the human body but are essential for many functions.
- Vitamins
- Minerals
- Water

Energy is measured in K calories
The energy released from the energy-yielding nutrients can be measured in calories, tiny units of energy so small that a simple apple provides tens of thousands of them. To ease calculations, energy is expressed in 1,000 calorie units known as kilocalories or kcalories, but is commonly referred just to as calories.
Example: 1 medium apple contains 100 calories or kcalories, a slice of bread has about 70-100 calories.

Energy Content in Foods
The energy content of a food depends on how much carbohydrate, fat and protein it contains. Each one yields differing amounts of energy as follows:
1 gram of carbohydrate = 4 calories (kilocalories) of energy.
1 gram of protein = 4 calories (kilocalories) of energy.
1 gram of fat = 9 calories (kilocalories) of energy.
1 gram of alcohol = 7 calories (kilocalories) of energy

Most foods contain all three energy-yielding nutrients, as well as water, vitamins, minerals, and other substances.

Most foods contain all three energy-yielding nutrients, as well as water, vitamins, minerals and may contain other substances like fiber. One of the nutrients is usually predominant, such as carbohydrates in bread. The body can make some of the needed nutrients, but others must come from the foods that we eat. They are known as essential nutrients. The food that we eat fuels all of life's activities.

How to Calculate the Energy Available from Foods?

Multiply the number of grams of carbohydrate, protein, and fat by the kcalories of energy they produce: 4, 4, or 9.

Add the results together:

For example: 1 slice of bread and 1 Tablespoon of peanut butter –

16 grams' carbohydrate	x	4 kcalories	= 64 kcalories
7 grams of protein	x	4 kcalories	= 28 kcalories
9 grams of fat	x	9 kcalories	= 81 kcalories

Total amount of kcalories in the bread and peanut butter   = 173 kcalories

You can calculate the percentage of kcalories that each type of nutrient contributes to the total. The percentage of kcalories for fat, for example, would be found by dividing the 81 fat kcalories by the total amount of calories.

   81 divided by 173 = 0.468 round up to 0.47

Now multiply by 100 to get the percentage:

   0.47 x 100 = 47 %

Health recommendations urge people to limit their daily intake of fats to less than 30%. However, this refers to the daily intake and not an individual food. Knowing the percentages of kcalories in foods helps people to adjust their intake accordingly throughout the day and make wise choices.

Summary of Benefits of a Vegetarian Diet
- Offers a wide variety of nutrients: vitamins and minerals and little fat.
- Reduces obesity.
- Reduces chronic disease: hypertension, heart disease, and cancer.
- Improves immune system.

Benefits upon the cardiovascular system:
- Zero cholesterol.
- Lower in total fat, and saturated fat which can increase cholesterol.
- High in phytosterols that block cholesterol absorption.
- High in potassium (protects from high blood pressure & onset of kidney disease)
- High in arginine, an amino acid that makes nitric oxide. In moderation, nitric oxide helps the blood vessels to open up.
- High in soluble fiber which helps.

- Lowers high cholesterol.
- Stabilizes blood sugar.
- Provide ample antioxidants.
- Promotes weight control.

Benefits on the Brain
- Provides a steady supply of glucose to the brain.
- Provides many antioxidants that protect nerve cells.
- Balances the electrical activity within the brain. Helps the frontal lobe to be in control rather than the hypothalamus.
- 50% less incidence of Alzheimer's disease.
- Keeps the arteries to the brain clean.
- Lowers the incidence of hypertension. High blood pressure destroys white matter in the brain.
- Helps to provide the correct balance of fatty acids in the membranes of the nerve cells.
- Assists in self-control.
- Less inflammatory chemicals.

Cancer related consideration
- Reduces the risk of cancer due to high intake of fruits and vegetables (phytochemicals).
- Colon cancer is notably less in vegetarians (Colon cancer victims usually eat high protein, high fat, and low fiber).
- SDA's have a significantly lower mortality rate from cancer than the rest of the population.

Other benefits
- Loaded with phytochemicals, substances in plant (other than nutrients) which protect the health.
- Less risk of stroke.
- Less problems with asthma (less additives and preservatives).
- Less symptoms & pain from rheumatoid arthritis.

Quotes:
CD 15: Only one lease of life is granted us; and the inquiry with everyone should be, 'How can I invest my powers so that they may yield the greatest profit? How can I do most for the glory of God and the benefit of my fellow men?

CD 20: Health is a treasure. Of all temporal possessions it is the most precious. Wealth, learning, and honor are dearly purchased at the loss of the vigor of health. None of these can secure happiness, if health is lacking.

CD 18: To keep the body in a healthy condition, in order that all parts of the living machinery may act harmoniously, should be a study of our life.

CD 21: Knowledge must be gained in regard to how to eat, and drink, and dress so as to preserve health.

CD 17: The Creator of man has arranged the living machinery of our bodies. Every function is wonderfully and wisely made. And God pledged Himself to keep this human machinery in healthful action if the human agent will obey His laws and cooperate with God.

CD 24: Seventh-day Adventists are handling momentous truths…As a people, we should make advancement proportionate to the light received. It is our duty to understand and respect the principles of health reform.

CD 24: Let those who are teachers and leaders in our cause take their stand firmly on Bible ground in regard to health reform and give a straight testimony to those who believe we are living in the last days of this earth's history.

National Research Council, Diet and Health, National Academy Press, 1989, p. 49.
The Holy Bible, King James Version, Nelson Publishers 686, Isaiah 55:2.
S. Williams, Nutrition and Diet Therapy, Mosby 7th Edition, 1989, pp 4,5.
William Dysinger, M.D., Heaven's Lifestyle Today, Review & Herald, 1997, pp.21,29,30.
Whitney, Cataldo, & Rolfes, Understanding Normal and Clinical Nutrition, 5th Edition, Wadsworth, 1998, pp. 4, 5
Whitney, Castaldo & Rolfes, Understanding Normal and Clinical Nutrition, Wadsworth, 5th Edition, p. 8
http://www.greenmuze.com/blogs/natural-notes/1098-health-benefits-of-parsley.html
This article from http://www.naturalnews.com/029346_parsley_vitamins.html

---

i. National Research Council, Diet and Health, National Academy Press, 1989, p. 49.

ii. The Holy Bible, King James Version, Nelson Publishers 686, Isaiah 55:2.

iii. William Dysinger, M.D., Heaven's Lifestyle Today, Review & Herald, 1997, pp.21,29,30.

iv. Whitney, Cataldo, & Rolfes, Understanding Normal and Clinical Nutrition, 5th Edition, Wadsworth, 1998, pp. 4,5